Scaling your OKR program

BASTIN GERALD

WITH SENTHIL RAJAGOPALAN

9 781794 812031

Table of Contents

Introduction

OKRs implemented the right way can be highly rewarding for teams and businesses. They can increase visibility for everyone, create an agile working environment, drive you to achieve stretch goals, and help you build high performance teams. The first two books in this *OKR Program* series, *Planning for your OKR Program* and *Launching your OKR Program*, covered the foundational aspects of an OKR program. This book, *Scaling your OKR Program*, is the third and final book in this series.

At this point, you have planned your OKR program well, launched OKRs for your first few business units, and have successfully completed the first quarter. Now, it's time to scale up and roll out to the rest of the organization; and this book can help.

Here, you will learn the ways that you can schedule your quarter with OKRs, prioritize your goals, use OKRs to create a learning organization, maintain best practices throughout your OKR program, and the signs and signals you must watch out for to determine if your OKR program is headed off track, or on the path towards success.

This book is filled with practical advice that you can put to work today. The OKR calendar suggested in *Chapter 1: What should your OKR quarter look like?* is a great template for you to create your own customized OKR quarterly calendar for your organization. *Chapter 3: How do you prioritize your OKRs*, provides a great framework to help you choose the right objectives and Key Results. *Chapter 7: What is Organizational Learning and Why is it Important?* introduces the concept of learning organization and provides the guidelines for using your OKR program to build a learning organization.

The advice found in this book has helped hundreds of OKR implementations across the globe. Many have been spectacularly successful while some have missed the initial ambitious goals. We have synthesized the valuable lessons learned from these experiences into the last two chapters with treasured insights on the *signs of a successful OKR implementation* as well as the *red flags*. We wish you amazing success with your OKR program.

1

What should your OKR quarter look like?

An OKR quarter can be well-structured and consistent when you have a very mature OKR program.

The phrase *mature OKR program* implies that if you're in your first quarter using OKRs, you probably will not see this strong structure. In fact, it may be two or three quarters before your company's culture and your team dynamics adjust to using OKRs as your main way to determine business health and progress.

What would this mature OKR structure look like? While nothing about the OKR framework is one size fits all, there are a handful of recommendations that can improve your experience implementing and managing OKRs.

Scheduling your Quarter with OKRs

You can use these schedule suggestions (Figure 1.1) as a starting point and tweak them to your preferences.

Your quarter using OKRs can look like this:

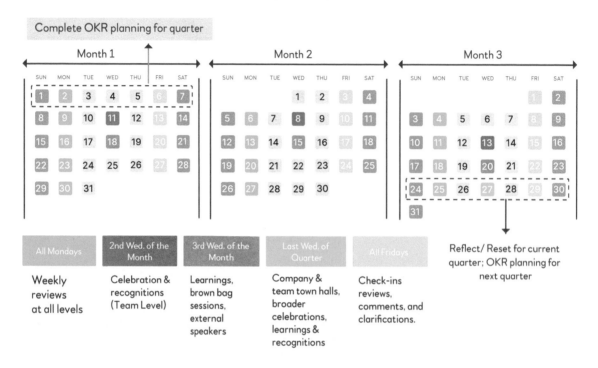

Figure 1.1: *A suggested starting point for how to bring the OKR framework into your quarterly schedule. This breakdown can be adjusted by OKR champions as their teams get used to the cadence of OKRs.*

To help you understand what you must include in your quarterly calendar for a successful OKR calendar, let's organize the key dates in this calendar around the PEEL cycle. The four stages of the PEEL cycle are:

- Plan

- Execute

- Engage

- Learn

Plan

All companies should kick off their quarter with a planning session. Taking an entire month to plan your quarter's OKRs would be a disaster. Ideally, your plan for the quarter should be in place by the end of your first week.

Now, this could seem very idealistic and not practical, especially when you are at the beginning of your OKR journey. For some teams, it's achievable, and for others it's not. However, it's a good goal to strive towards.

It might take two, three, or four quarters for your team to plan their OKRs within a week. The more planning cycles your team goes through, the easier it will be to identify the quarter's most important priorities. This process will eventually feel business-as-usual, and your team will be able to set and align OKRs in the first week without issue.

Execute

Throughout the quarter, you should schedule weekly or biweekly check-ins. These will typically take place on Fridays as a summary of your week as a whole. While you can set check-ins at any cadence and on any day that suits your company's needs, you must keep check-ins consistent. OKR champions and business leaders should stress the importance of updating key result progress, status, and writing comments every week.

You can use the **PPP framework** or something similar to structure your reporting. The PPP framework asks users to record the progress, plans, and problems faced while working on their key result during the last check-in period. Structuring reviews around these three components will help users hit on all of the important information associated with their key result and keep check-ins informative and to the point.

Engage

Once check-ins are completed, they should be reviewed by managers and stakeholders to understand so everyone is up to date on the latest key result progress. Teams should also discuss the plan for each week and the roadblocks they are facing while making progress on key results.

Check-ins, commentaries, and reports can be reviewed on Mondays. When your organization has multiple levels in the business, you can split up your review meetings in groups. Ask team leaders to hold lower-level team meetings individually to discuss check-ins in-depth and work through important problems as a unit. Then, at the higher-level team meetings, ensure that everyone has a chance to update the entire group with a shorter summary of what was accomplished and what plans and problems people have. This helps maintain full transparency throughout the business and keep the team aligned without glossing over any important issues with brief big-picture meetings.

On the calendar shown above (Fig. 1.1), these reviews happen each Monday. Like check-ins, this cadence can be adjusted to fit the exact needs of your team.

1-on-1s between managers and their direct reports should focus on OKRs. When your team has their focus trained on OKRs, you can quickly learn what is working, what is not, and what needs to be done to help your team members accomplish their targets.

OKR-focused meetings make conversations more meaningful. While you want your team members to get things done, there can be a lot of "points of failure" that need to be addressed along the way. When you have check-ins cataloguing what has been tried and didn't work, you can provide meaningful guidance or appropriate help efficiently.

Additionally, it's wise to use your second Wednesdays of the month for celebrations and recognitions. These celebrations can be localized at the team or department level.

These meetings should have an agenda and have a standard process for recognizing great work.

Once per quarter, you should hold a broader business unit or company-level town hall meeting. In this calendar, the standard day is Wednesday (Fig. 1.1). However, you can choose any day that works for you. During these last Wednesdays, you can have a company-level State-of-the-union or a business-unit-level State-of-the-union.

Have the appropriate C-suite executives share their updates as needed. You can certainly run through your company-level OKRs and where you stand while you are wrapping your quarter as well as share the company-level priorities for the next quarter.

You can also have broader celebrations, broader learning, and recognition at the large department, business unit, or company-level as appropriate. It's tough to have a company level State-of-the-union every quarter if your company is large, but you have to work through and figure out what is best for your organization's culture, size, and OKR cadence.

Learn

Learning should be a big part of your company's OKR culture. You can dedicate the third Wednesday of the month to learning.

Apart from your team members sharing their learnings in these sessions, you can supplement your learning culture by:

- Gathering customer feedback about what worked well, what didn't, and what could have worked better

- Invite industry experts to speak to your team and share expertise related to what you are trying to accomplish

Whether these learning sessions take place at the business unit level, department level, or team level is entirely up to you to decide based on your company's needs. However, it's important to have a day dedicated to learning and growing as a company. Learning is a vital component of success with the OKR framework.

While learning should be a part of your weekly routine, you should also go through a longer reflection process at the very end of each quarter. This process collates the information and learnings you've gathered each week and asks users to consider their OKR progress.

Many businesses with mature OKR programs take a few weeks to complete the Reflect/Reset process at the end of the quarter. So, you won't be alone if you take a few weeks to get this done appropriately. It's important not to rush through this learning process, and you should aim to complete your reflect/reset process in one or two weeks.

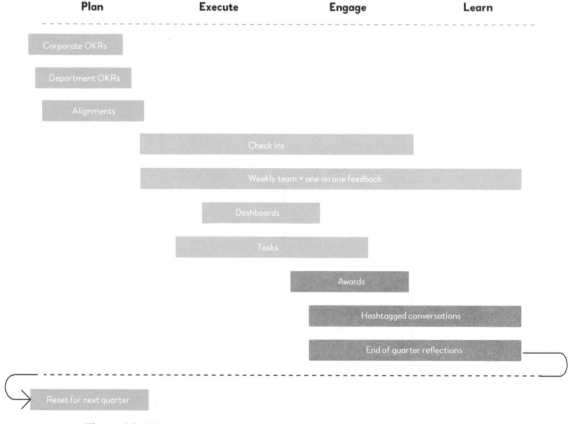

Figure 1.2: *This image demonstrates how the PEEL cycle fits into your OKR quarter, and how the "learning" stage of the process links directly to the "planning" stage.*

The learning stage of the PEEL cycle connects directly with the planning stage of your next quarter. During the reflection process, where you record what you've learned throughout the quarter, you will also reset your OKRs or extend existing OKRs into the next quarter. OKRs for the following quarter should always be well-informed by your past experience, linking the "learn" and "plan" phases of the PEEL cycle (Fig. 1.2).

Final Thoughts

Keep in mind that the calendar shown in this chapter is simply a starting point for your individualized OKR program (Fig. 1.1). Your own quarterly OKR calendar will be influenced by your organizational culture, structure, and business processes. So, your calendar will reflect the specifics of your organization in some way, shape, or form.

Get started with the basics presented here, and modify and adapt as needed in your organization. For example, some companies might elect to set OKRs on an annual basis rather than a quarterly one, or check-in cadences will be bi-weekly rather than weekly. Every choice your organization makes for its OKR program will make your quarter with OKRs look different— the most important thing is that the leadership team is dedicating time and effort to ingraining this strategy-execution framework into the DNA of your company.

What should your OKR quarter look like?

2

How do you ensure that your OKRs are good, at scale?

Objectives and Key Results (OKR) software, when correctly deployed, is a powerful tool that can be used to guide an organization towards success. However, the way that the OKR software industry has evolved has caused many company leaders to approach the framework with many preconceived notions.

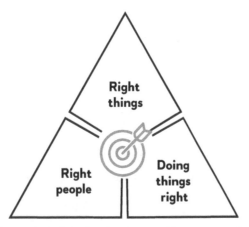

Figure 2.1: *An image depicting what it takes to achieve your goals using the OKR framework; you must focus on the right things, with the right people, who do things right.*

These notions include the idea that OKRs are synonymous with task management or performance management. Both of these perceptions can cause issues with a company's OKR implementation.

One question that many individuals new to OKRs ask is: *"Will OKRs improve the performance of underperforming teams or underperforming employees?"*

Can OKRs boost the performance of underperforming teams and employees?

It is a common question many people ask when testing waters with OKRs. It's important to note that the OKR framework isn't a performance management methodology. However, OKRs can be used to help employees make better use of their time, effort, and skill. OKRs are a great way to get the most out of your team and therefore improve performance— but the approach you take to this performance improvement is very important.

The Business Process Equation

From a bird's eye view, a business has several core business processes, as well as a set of tools to create output. These outputs, in turn, lead to meaningful outcomes for the business.

Many business leaders are eager to learn about OKRs and performance improvement because many of us are biased towards **outputs** or **inputs**. Leaders tend to wonder if they have the right people, and if those people are doing the right tasks.

However, success is about more than inputs and outputs. All successful organizations realize

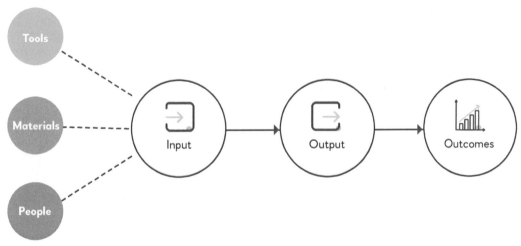

Figure 2.2: This is the business process equation, which demonstrates how tools, materials, and people eventually lead to outcomes for a business.

at some point in their evolution that measuring the journey is a critical component of ensuring timely and cost-effective arrival at their intended destination. This has resulted in a market chock-full of software that helps organizations track progress and process. However, not all measuring tools (software or methodologies) are created equal.

If a business leader is in a rush to implement a framework like OKRs, find software for their team, and improve performance, they will likely be disappointed. Selecting a tool that isn't right for your team can have a negative impact on your experience with OKRs, and focusing on the wrong aspects of goal-setting and tracking can lead to underwhelming results.

What happens when you are focused on Output?

Consider the following scenario:

A finance director is monitoring the activities of his credit control team using a software dashboard. The actions of each credit controller are broken down into measurable tasks. In theory, each task triggers another task that should lead to effective credit control management and help the organization's overall cash flow. The cash position of the organization is a significant focus of the executive team.

They have a few hundred medium-sized clients with varying degrees of late payments. The dashboard shows that all tasks are completed. Despite the dashboard's promise that the company is checking all the right boxes, the organization still struggles with significant cash flow problems.

In this hypothetical example, the cause of this cash issue is that the company manages one large client outside the purview of the credit control team. This one client accounts for 50% of the organization's problem debt. However, because the dashboard is geared towards measuring outputs and tasks, the management team misses this detail and is left scratching their heads. While this example might seem extreme and easily mitigated by effective management communication and cross-functional collaboration, it is often not as simple as that to fix.

Larger organizations usually have more elaborate silos and departmental structures than smaller businesses. Therefore, they are more dependent on systems and reporting to inform the executive team of team progress towards the company's mission.

The finance team can happily report that it is meeting or exceeding its performance standards, and all tasks are being conducted according to the plan. Regardless, the company will still struggle. Companies that focus on output alone aren't solving the issues in their organization, or setting themselves up for success with OKRs.

What happens when you focus on Employees?

To understand the dangers of hastily-implemented OKR solutions, let's look at another example.

Our cash-strapped client in the previous example has shifted their focus from tasks to the people responsible for keeping credit risk under control. The organization took the view that a task focus had not delivered the right data framework, and they are now hoping for a more active approach.

This time, the approach is more biased towards employee development. There is a heavy emphasis on skill alignment and ensuring that goals are cascaded down from the executive leadership team to individual team members.

This sounds great in theory. The problem is that the very same issues exist with this approach as with the previous task focus. They are just masquerading under a different set of metrics. Developing an employee's skill set sounds like an arguably good idea.

Yet, it does not take too much creativity to imagine why it could be extremely counterproductive to focus only on employees' skills without a holistic data set.

Let's assume that our example company has an ambitious expansion plan. Their path to success is deemed to be mostly dependent upon the performance of the field sales team that was inherited from a recent merger.

The data suggests that this team is collectively underperforming in a specific part of the sales cycle. Human resources acts upon this data and recommends an aggressive and expansive learning and development program to upskill the team.

Nothing about this so far should seem particularly controversial. Yet, just like in the credit control example, the metrics fail to identify that training is not the right way to see rapid improvement.

In this particular example, the incumbent sales organization was made up of expensive field agents, and the company would have been better served by replacing them with high-volume, lower cost telesales specialists.

Both of these examples are relatively simplistic, and one would hope that any organization would be able to avoid these issues. And yet, because large organizations can become so complex, problems with simple solutions can be unidentifiable.

These are examples of how data can be misleading when the OKR framework has been constructed around the wrong focus.

The larger and more complex an organization gets, the more important it is for teams to use the OKR framework and their chosen OKR software correctly.

Where in this equation do you set your OKRs?

You can set OKRs for any stage of the business process equation: outcomes, outputs, inputs, and even the individual input components.

But the best OKRs address the right side of this equation: the outcomes.

Instead of saying, *"I want to improve the performance of my underperforming employees,"* set goals to improve them. Alternatively, set OKRs that will focus on the outcomes they produce.

For example, say you operate a network operations center (NOC), and you feel that the group is not working out well. Instead of focusing on how many tickets each employee in the group closes, which is a good indication of their output, set key results that focus on uptime, reducing repeated tickets, and so on.

Focusing on the outcomes, rather than outputs, helps clarify the true goals of the team. There is no ambiguity. Either you achieved them, or you didn't. Good outcomes are most certainly influenced by good outputs, which in turn are the result of good inputs.

But sometimes, it might be harder to set your Key Results based on outcomes. In those cases, focus on output rather than the inputs.

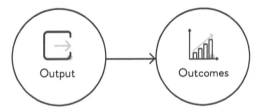

For example, instead of asking a call center agent to work 8 hours, ask them to make 100 calls a day. If you know that an average agent can generate five leads for every 100 calls, this will ensure you are getting the most out of that employee.

Business Process Interactions

Processes do not exist in isolation. There are many interconnections between processes. One process's output or outcome will be the input for another process.

For example, the outcome of the *"lead generation"* process is *"qualified leads." "Qualified leads"* is the input to the *"sales process."* You will have to visualize this interconnection, understand the different outcomes, and set Key Results for the appropriate people based on that. For example, take a look at the sales process represented in figure 2.3.

Figure 2.3: The business process for finding and signing on new clients.
This process involves three departments: marketing, sales, and account management

You can see that there are three different groups involved in this process: **Marketing, Sales, and Account Management**.

Marketing runs campaigns that result in MQLs, or marketing qualified leads.

Those then become general SQLs, or sales qualified leads, which become sales opportunities when the sales team is able to close the deal. Those deals become orders, and so on.

As you can see, one group or function's outcome is typically input to another function (Fig. 2.3). To balance this interconnected process, leaders must select their KPIs carefully and think through the process as they define their OKRs.

The Business Process Equation Perspective & Different Types of KRs

Writing effective key results involves a lot of forethought and consideration. Taking multiple perspectives when formulating key results is a wise tactic if you're looking to get the best results from your OKR program. Many terms regarding key results have been mentioned in this OKR Program series. Let's quickly review these for clarity.

Key result *types* are the seven ways you can measure your key results. These include percentage tracked, milestone tracked, task tracked, baseline KPI, control KPI, increase KPI, and decrease KPI key results. Next, there are key result *classes*. A key result's class is the defining factor that explains how it functions in your OKR. These four key result classes are leading indicator KPI, lagging indicator KPI, activity-based, and paired or balanced key results. Finally, there are key result *categories*; these categories will be discussed below. These are defined from the perspective of the business process equation, and are input, output, and outcome key results.

In the second installment of this *OKR Program series, Launching Your OKR Program*, the four classes of key results and the different OKR levels they were usually set at were discussed. These four classes were lagging indicator key results, leading indicator key results, activity-based key results, and balancing or paired key results. These four classes were discussed in detail in chapter three of the book *Launching Your OKR Program*, but let's quickly recap:

First, lagging indicator KRs are key results based on KPIs that measure the most important targets for a business' goal, but also something that you don't know until the end of the measurement period. For example, if an objective is to *Grow Revenue,* a lagging indicator key result would be "Increase expansion revenue from $0M to $4M." Next is a leading indicator key result. This is a key result that is measured using a KPI that directly affects the business's goal; for example, with the Objective of *Grow Revenue*, a leading indicator key result would be "Increase the demo to contract conversion rate from 20% to 40%" because this conversion rate will lead to an increase in revenue. Activity based key results are measured using output, such as completed tasks or initiatives. Finally, balancing or paired key results serve to balance our growth targets with targets that address maintaining quality and keeping customers satisfied.

The Input, Output, and Outcome key result categories introduced in this book are connected with the four key result classes outlined in *Launching your OKR Program*. To understand the relationship between these key result categories and classes, take a look at figure 2.4.

	Input KRs	Output KRs	Outcome KRs
Lagging Indicator KRs			X
Leading Indicator KRs	X	X	
Activity-Based KRs	X	X	
Balancing or Paired KRs	X	X	X

Figure 2.4: A matrix outlining the relationship between the four classes of key results, shown on the four rows, and the three categories of key results, shown on the columns.

This matrix shows how each class of key results falls into the three categories: Input, Output, or Outcome. As we know, the distribution of the key result classes changes based on the OKR level. Now, let's reconcile these key result classes from the perspective of the business process equation.

First, lagging indicators will usually be outcome key results. These key results address the end of the business process equation, and measure tangible KPIs that are usually apparent indicators of the measured objective. You could attempt to control the input or output of these key results, but those would be deemed "leading indicator key results". For example, if your goal is to sell more of a product, you might want to create a better product. The outcome would be an increase in sales, which is a lagging indicator. But the leading indicator would be the inputs and outputs. As you know, the quality of inputs on the business process equation directly affects the quality of outputs. If you are creating a product, and the quality of your supplier's materials is very good, you can create a good product— your input and output, the leading indicators— and in turn sell more of that product— your outcome, or your lagging indicator.

Third is activity-based key results. Since these key results measure work that you perform, these key results are also input or output-focused. Inputs might be the number of hours that employees work, or the time spent creating a product. Output addresses the result of those hours put in.

Finally, balancing or paired KRs can be in any of the three key result categories: input, output, or outcome key results. These key results ensure that you don't have tunnel-vision. These could fall at any point of the business process equation.

The Google Problem

Knowing the difference between inputs, outputs, and outcomes— and which ones you should measure— is an important part of maintaining the quality and relevance of your OKRs. You have to make sure that your OKRs make sense for the specific business function you are working with. Additionally, you need to make sure there's a culture match between the types of OKRs you set, and the team you're setting them for.

To understand the importance of this step, consider the tech titan Google.

Google is one of the most well-known proponents of the OKR framework's merits, proudly utilizing it as a methodology to drive success. However, using Google as a case study for OKR best practices carries any number of challenges for those organizations seeking to emulate their success. Consider this statement from Don Dodge in 2010 about the way Google sets and tracks its goals:

"Achieving 65% of the impossible is better than 100% of the ordinary"

Organizations have adopted this as their goal-setting mantra within their OKR programs. It's another version of the *"Shoot for the moon, and even if you miss, you'll land among the stars"* philosophy.

At first glance, this might seem like a credible and praiseworthy approach. Yet, unchecked, this Google goal philosophy may do more harm than good within an organization.

Think about an organization that may have evolved with well moderated, conservative, and regularly achievable goals. A team that's used to seeing 100% OKR progress each quarter might become disillusioned when they are suddenly underachieving on all of their goals.

Committing to such an ambitious goal-setting technique before employees have been properly trained on the rules of the framework is a gamble. A misguided software vendor might encourage one method that is completely out of alignment with the company's culture. A workforce that has become used to receiving praise for 100% goal attainment may not feel that "*65% of the impossible*" is a success, and might lose steam before they can even reach that threshold.

The GLUT Effect

What do Google, LinkedIn, Uber, and Twitter have in common?

Aside from being category giants within their industries, they are all famously passionate advocates of OKRs.

These companies all have robust OKR programs that are often used as models for other organizations to aspire to.

Is this a problem? Potentially yes.

The GLUT companies indeed adopted OKR software in extremely effective ways, but they had many additional and arguably unrepeatable factors perpetuating their success.

The OKR approaches that worked for these high-profile companies won't necessarily work for your organization. When setting goals, selecting an OKR vendor, and implementing the framework, you need to have a consultative approach to find out what will work best for your organization. Consider the size, culture, and history of OKRs in your organization instead of simply taking a cue from companies like Google, LinkedIn, Uber, and Twitter.

Final Thoughts

OKRs, when implemented correctly, provide accurate, objective measurements to an organization's decision-makers. OKRs should empower stakeholders, and give a clear picture of the targets that must be reached.

Software vendors in the OKR market do not always present OKRs in this light. Many companies approach OKRs with pre-existing biases due to a software geared towards tracking solely inputs or outputs. Focusing on these aspects of an organization alone will skew the accuracy of the software, and the effectiveness of OKRs.

So, it's important to dedicate focus to the right side of this business process equation whenever you can. You will bring in a very positive, outcome-oriented culture that focuses on business results instead of worrying about making people work harder or smarter.

Show employees what you want to achieve, and outline the bigger picture and what waits for them when they get there. You will see everyone giving their best effort to get there when you focus on outcomes and empower employees with the right tools and support.

How do you ensure that your OKRs are good, at scale?

3

How do you prioritize your OKRs?

Prioritizing is critical to the success of any business endeavor. There are always going to be problems competing for your full attention, and you need to be able to identify which ones are more important.

Shooting for the moon is an enormous endeavor. When you shoot for the moon, you must ensure that you'll last long enough to see that day when you get to the moon. So, the success of an optimized business rests heavily on identifying the right priorities.

> *If I were given one hour to save the planet, I would spend 59 minutes defining the problem and one minute resolving it.*

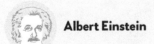 **Albert Einstein**

Albert Einstein once said, "If I were given one hour to save the planet, I would spend 59 minutes defining the problem and one minute resolving it." This approach is critical as understanding the problem and its causality is the first step to solving it.

How do OKRs factor into solving business problems? Objectives define what you want the future state of your company to be, after the problem is solved. Meanwhile, the key results measure the progress or outcomes you need to see along the journey.

Prioritizing Objectives

As a first step towards having the right list of OKRs, you must prioritize your objectives first and then the key results within each objective.

There are five buckets your objectives can fall into in the prioritization process:

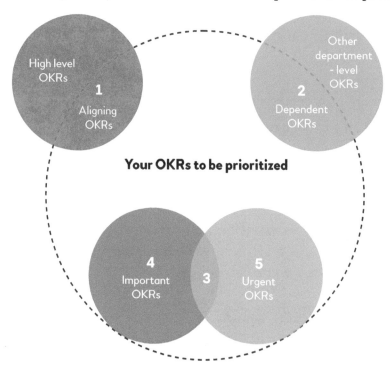

Figure 3.1: This diagram illustrates how you should prioritize your OKRs within a quarter.

- Aligning OKRs

- Dependent OKRs.

- Important and Urgent OKRs.

- Important, but not Urgent OKRs.

- Urgent, but not important OKRs.

#1– Aligning OKRs

First and foremost, you should prioritize objectives by aligning them within your organization—especially between your corporate and department-level OKRs. You have to trust your direct reports, right? If you have misalignment concerns, you have to make a point to resolve any confusion before you launch into the quarter.

The same applies if you are an employee with individual OKRs, and you notice that your OKRs are out of alignment with departmental OKRs. You will have to have an open discussion with your direct supervisors. Aligned OKRs are naturally top-priority OKRs, because they contribute to other, larger goals in the company that must be completed.

#2– Dependent OKRs

Once you have taken care of the "aligning objectives," you should look at the non-aligning ones. While there are a few ways you can prioritize these OKRs, keep in mind that everyone is ultimately working towards fulfilling company objectives. With that end goal in mind, you should be helping other departments achieve OKRs that need your contribution in order to hit higher-level targets.

So, once your aligned OKRs are fulfilled, move on to your OKRs that other stakeholders in your organization are depending on in order to find success. Although the diagram shown in figure 3.1 shows that circles #1 and #2 do not necessarily overlap, they certainly can, as you might have dependencies with OKRs that align upwards.

#3– Important & Urgent OKRs

Once you have addressed both aligned OKRs and dependent OKRs, you can focus on independent OKRs for your department and then prioritize those using the **Importance vs. Urgency Matrix.**

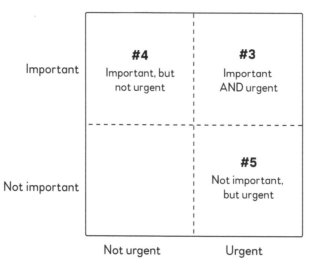

Figure 3.2: *This is the Importance vs. Urgency Matrix, illustrating how you should prioritize OKRs that fall into one of the three numbered quadrants of the grid.*

As you can see from the Action Prioritization Matrix above, your objectives can fall into 4 different quadrants:

- Not Important and Not Urgent.

- Not Important, but Urgent.

- Important, but Not Urgent.

- Important AND Urgent.

After aligning and dependent objectives are taken care of, you should prioritize objectives that are in the **Important & Urgent** quadrant. While the prioritization of goals that fall on this matrix might seem straightforward, many companies tend to fulfill what is most urgent without thinking about the importance or impact of a goal.

The default method of prioritizing objectives might differ from industry-to-industry. For example, for manufacturing companies, quality is a vital objective that will not always align with other goals within the company. According to the quality-first principle that many organizations practice, "Improve Quality" would be an essential objective, as well as an urgent one (as emphasized by the word "first" or "foremost" by many businesses.)

#4– Important, but not Urgent Objectives

Next, prioritize important, but not urgent objectives. To understand what this type of OKR might look like, let's look at an example scenario.

Let's say you know that you have to get a solid outbound marketing program going. But you still need to perfect your inbound marketing before focusing on outbound, because of resource constraints. Such a goal would fall under the "Important, but Not Urgent" category. While this goal isn't necessarily under a time constraint and may not seem as urgent as your outbound program, not fulfilling it will have negative impacts on your business down the line.

#5– Urgent, but unimportant Objectives

Lastly, prioritize OKRs that are urgent, but unimportant. In every quarter with OKRs, there are always projects and targets that need to be taken care of right away.

For example, you might be a Sales leader, and it is important to prepare Sales forecasts for an upcoming meeting. However, it is the end of the quarter, and your team needs your help in closing pending deals (which are both Important and Urgent). So, you will spend more time helping your team close deals. While the Sales forecasts do need to be completed, the OKR program asks you to consider the impact and outcomes of each project you prioritize.

Prioritizing Key Results within an Objective

Now that we've established how you should prioritize your OKRs in broad strokes, let's take a look at specific key result prioritization.

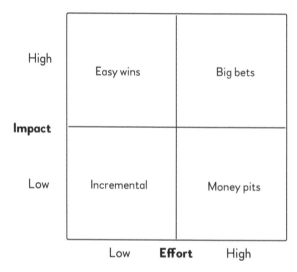

Figure 3.3: This matrix shows the impact and effort of key results. The four quadrants that this matrix creates should be used to determine if a key result is worth including in a given quarter or on an OKR.

As you can see from the Action Prioritization Matrix above, your key results can fall into four categories as represented by the four quadrants:

- Easy Wins

- Big Bets

- Incremental

- Money Pits

#1. Easy Wins

An Easy Win is a key result that demands minimal effort, but gives you a big bang for your buck.

For example, a key result of "Increase the number of page visits to 500" will result from a high-quality content strategy. The effort required is low, but the impact will be high. Give these key results a higher priority.

#2. Big Bets

Key results that take much effort but are also highly impactful for your company are called Big Bets. For example, a key result such as "Increase the number of leads to 500" is a big bet towards increased revenue generation.

#3. Incremental

This section is for low effort and low impact key results. For example, refreshing your web pages is low effort, and might not have a considerable immediate impact, but the gains will compound over time.

#4. Money Pits

A key result that drains a lot of your energy or effort but only impacts your company marginally is called a Money Pit. For example, 'Redesign ad campaigns' may turn into a money pit when there is a resource shortage in your team. So, be aware of where key results could turn into money pits, and keep those outcomes on low priority.

So how do you balance the key results you have in a given quarter? Aim to pick out key results like this:

- As many "Quick Wins" as possible

- A couple of "Incrementals" per quarter

- 1-2 "Big Bets" per quarter.

- And no "Money Pits"

Teams should set three to five key results per objective. If you see an OKR that is an important objective followed by three money pit key results, you should step in and discuss the outcomes with your employees so that resources aren't squandered on high-effort, low impact items.

The Success of your OKRs Depends on Prioritization

The success of your OKRs relies heavily on your ability to **Focus.** To maximize focus, prioritization is essential. Knowing what and how to prioritize is the key to a successful OKR program.

How do you know if you have picked your key results correctly?

Let us use an example and understand if the key results you have come up with are the right ones. In this example, the team is trying to reduce the page load time of a web page, to keep in line with Google's recommendations for webmasters.

It is now well-known that "page load time" is one of the key factors for successful SEO. Apart from SEO considerations, page loading time is also a critical aspect from a UX standpoint.

Once this is decided as an important enough KPI to address, the engineering and the website teams work together and come back with five key results. Let's take a look at this particular OKR:

- KR1: Compress the CSS and JavaScript files to improve page performance

- KR2: Compress images for better page performance

- KR3: Remove unwanted JavaScript files in web and mobile view

- KR4: Decrease page loading time from 10,000 milliseconds to 500 milliseconds

- KR5: Decrease the number of HTTP requests from 50 to 25

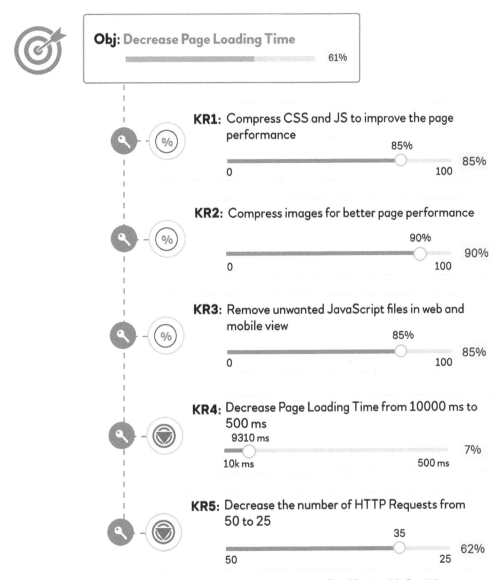

Figure 3.4: An OKR to "Decrease Page Loading Time" with five KRs.

Let us say that both the Marketing and Engineering teams have approved this, and have started executing on this Objective.

Three weeks into the cycle, you check in to see the progress of these key results. However, while you notice substantial progress has been made for key results 1, 2, 3, and 5, the fourth key result is sitting around 7%. As the topical key result, this presents a big problem.

The problem is that you are not achieving the bottom-line impact that you were planning to accomplish by executing the other four key results.

During the planning process, this was overlooked, and the execution of the key result did not go well. During one of the weekly reviews, the manager noticed this lagging progress and adjusted the team's strategy.

Detecting this anomaly three weeks into the quarter is a lot better than completing the entire quarter only to realize that no progress was made on the key result that mattered most for the success of the objective.

It's important to detect errors like this one early so your team can course-correct and focus on what is most important. The OKR framework requires frequent check-ins, which help teams spot problems like this one.

As you can see from this two-by-two matrix (Fig. 3.5), there are two axes:

- Prioritization of Action Items on the Y-axis.

- Completeness of Analysis / Action Plan on the X-axis.

So, on each axis, there are two buckets. On the X-axis, completeness of action / analysis action plan, the range is from:

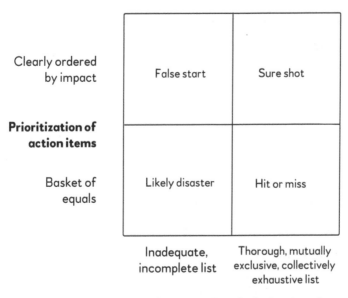

Figure 3.5: *A matrix illustrating how action items are prioritized against the completeness of the action plan.*

- Inadequate and incomplete list

to

- Mutually Exclusive and Collectively Exhaustive (MECE) list

On the Y-axis, prioritization of action items, the range goes from:

- Basket of Equals (the list of actions has not been prioritized properly)

to

- Clearly Ordered by Impact

Now, if you start with an Inadequate or Incomplete list and do not prioritize and treat your actions as a basket of equals, you have a disaster waiting to happen. Unless you are fortunate, you are not going to achieve your Key Result. It is plain and simple.

Let's say you have an Inadequate and Incomplete list, but then you try to order it by impact and begin. Even if you benefit from this progress, it is still a false start, because the key results are not measuring everything that needs to be included in order to properly fulfill the objective.

Now, take a look at the bottom half of the matrix (Fig. 3.5). Even if your key results follow the MECE rule, it still won't be a sure thing if you have not prioritized them properly. It will still be a hit or miss because depending on what you pick, you may not complete them if you cannot focus on what matters most.

Finally, there is the fourth quadrant. If you have a mutually exclusive, collectively exhaustive list of key results, which is clearly ordered by impact, this will give you a sure shot at achieving the objective you set out to fulfill.

Let's go back to the example OKR "Decrease Page Loading Time". This example suffers from an inadequate list problem. The team has made considerable progress on four of the five key results. However, there is nearly no impact on the fourth key result– to decrease page loading time from 10,000 ms to 500 ms– which is the key result that matters most for the achievement of the objective.

This tells you that the key results make up an incomplete list. So, this means you must go back and look for other things that need to be done, which will impact the bottom line.

Prioritization does not seem to be a problem here, because the list is small, but it could be a problem in other situations. This specific example is representative of a "False Start". Once you have the full list, you will know if you have a prioritization problem. The first order of business is to get the full list of key results, and then analyze your approach.

How do you prioritize your OKRs?

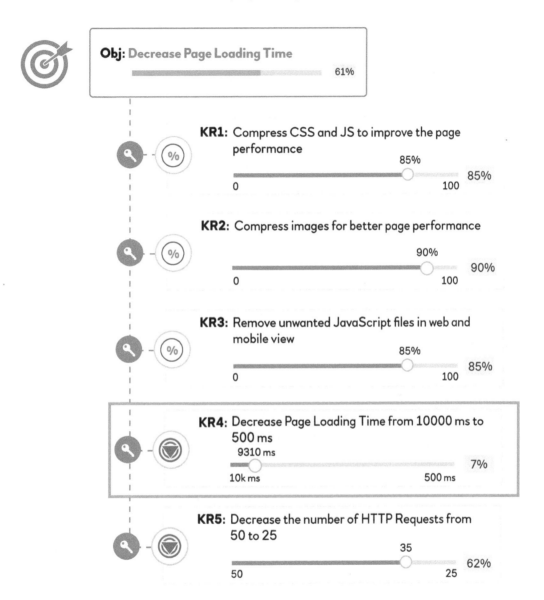

Obj: Decrease Page Loading Time — 61%

KR1: Compress CSS and JS to improve the page performance — 85% / 0–100 — 85%

KR2: Compress images for better page performance — 90% / 0–100 — 90%

KR3: Remove unwanted JavaScript files in web and mobile view — 85% / 0–100 — 85%

KR4: Decrease Page Loading Time from 10000 ms to 500 ms — 9310 ms / 10k ms – 500 ms — 7%

KR5: Decrease the number of HTTP Requests from 50 to 25 — 35 / 50 – 25 — 62%

How do you prioritize your OKRs?

.

4

How do you automate daily management?

OKRs are recommended for strategic and critical initiatives that move your business forward. These could include increasing annual revenue, signing 'X' number of enterprise clients, increasing NPS (Net Promoter Score), increasing department headcount, and many more initiatives.

Many OKR consultants mention that it's too difficult to manage the proliferation of OKRs when you try to expand the scope and application of OKRs beyond the essential key results.

Many leaders that are new to the OKR framework tend to wonder if they should push all of their OKRs down to the individual contributor level. How does it work?

In chapter two, we discussed the business process equation, and how you should aim to focus on business outcomes when setting your key results, rather than solely inputs or outputs. This is especially important for business leaders to consider.

You should move away from measuring employee effectiveness directly. Instead of counting an employees' daily tasks or the number of hours they are at their desk as a way to measure effectiveness, you should turn your attention to the business outcomes that you would see if your employees were operating at their best.

The problem is not that OKRs can't be applied at the operational level, it is merely that the management of those OKRs can lead to many frustrations.

Luckily, those frustrations can be solved with the help of good OKR software, especially if they can automate the *"management function"* associated with setting targets, tracking, reporting exceptions, and helping the OKR owner to achieve their goals. Therefore, OKRs at the operational level are a matter of feasibility, not applicability.

OKRs can not only become your daily management tool, but they can also help automate day-to-day management and take much management overhead out of the system.

How would you take OKRs to the operational level and reap the benefits of focus, alignment, commitment, tracking, and stretching?

Focus   Alignment   Commitment   Tracking   Stretching

Figure 4.1: The five elements or benefits of OKRs.

Let's look at an example to help illustrate this concept.

Say the marketing department wants to develop the lead flow process. To address this, you can have an objective at the marketing level to *Build a High-Quality Inbound Lead Pipeline*.

Now there could be key results at the strategic level that address:

- Generating product sign-ups
- Employing better tools
- Increase website visitors

The marketing department's OKR could be:

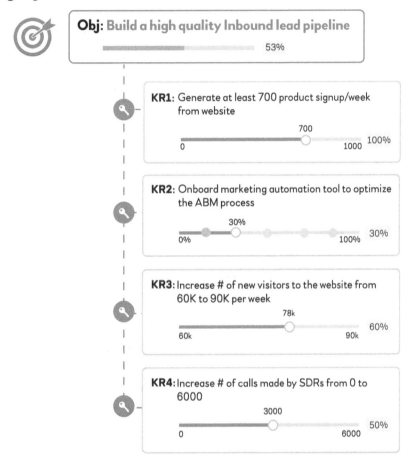

Let's take a closer look at the fourth key result: "Increase # of calls made by SDRs from 0 to 6000". When it comes to modeling this key result, you can take two different approaches:

- Using a percentage-tracked key result (from 0% progress to 100%), the SDR will have to calculate his or her achievement by individually tracking and updating progress during their check-ins.

- Using 'number of calls' as a tracked value, SDRs can check in their progress each week by counting up the number of calls they make, and reporting the number.

There is nothing blatantly wrong with this manner of tracking progress. However, there are better ways of approaching this key result.

A better way to track this key result is to set a Control KPI to maintain a number of 100 calls per day. The SDR will need to check in their activity on a daily basis.

As you can see from the graph in figure 4.2, this key result will have planned check-ins for the five weekdays. As long as the SDR stays at or above their target of 100 calls for each check-in, the key result will have 100% achievement.

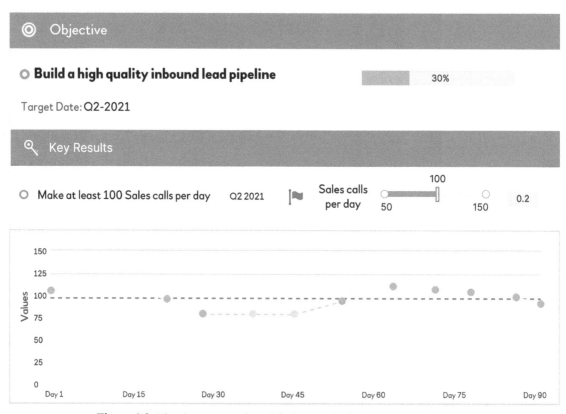

Figure 4.2: *Visual representation of the key result check-ins for the key result "Make at least 100 sales calls per day."*

Now it may not be feasible to hit the number '100', and that is perfectly fine in the OKR world. You should be setting ambitious targets that are just out of reach. If SDRs are achieving 75-80% of a stretch target, they are in good shape.

If your SDRs are tracking around 30-50% achievement, try to understand, analyze, and improve.

The idea is to track daily progress and inform an employee's daily functions. Daily management with OKRs requires software that allows your team to track key results in clear, straightforward ways. This will help your employees provide accurate and honest check-ins, and give managers the benefit of complete transparency into their team's daily activities. If they miss a check-in, it counts against them.

This way, the managers or supervisors do not have to follow-up with employees for daily reports– it is all available on one central platform.

How do you automate daily management?

5

When do you automate check-ins?

Check-ins are an integral part of the OKR process. Often, check-ins are thought of as merely updating the key result's progress value, and many companies want to automate check-ins rather than rely on employees to provide accurate data on time.

Automating check-ins isn't an uncommon practice, but it's not always the best course of action. Let's take a closer look at the nature of check-ins themselves, and when automation is appropriate.

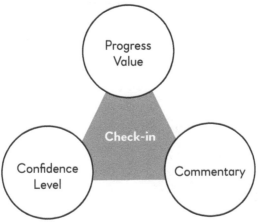

Figure 5.1: The three components of an informative check-in.

First of all, it's important to understand that check-ins usually consist of three parts:

- **Progress Value**: Numerical indication of how the key result has been progressing

- **Confidence Level**: The KR owner's confidence that they can achieve the target by the deadline

- **Commentary**: A brief description of progress, challenges, and outlook

As you can see, the data itself is just one single part of what a check-in is. If you would like, you can automate part one of your check-ins by connecting your OKR software with your data tracking platforms such as Google Sheets or Salesforce.

However, an automated check-in can't provide the information required of the second and third components of a check-in— both of which are just as, if not more, important than the value.

What are KPI Integrations?

KPI integrations refer to updating the KPI progress value associated with key results automatically through connections with transaction systems. Many companies pull this data from source systems such as Salesforce, Zendesk, Zoho, JIRA, Oracle ERP, and SAP.

So, instead of having key result owners hunt down accurate data across multiple platforms to get the most updated KPI values before a meeting, they can now automatically harvest those numbers and present them.

This helps employees save valuable time, and ensures that they have accurate and up-to-date data, leaving no room for data entry errors.

Two Schools of Thought

There are two schools of thought when it comes to automating KPI updates. These represent two extremes, and then most companies probably fall somewhere in between the two.

On one end of the spectrum, there's the belief that you should never automate check-ins. The thought is that OKR is a methodology and, at the same time, represents a mindset. Your key results must stay on your mind, because they're your most important priorities. Additionally, people emphasize the process element of OKRs themselves. Employees are supposed to look at the progress, comment on it, reflect on it, and articulate their future approach.

This emphasizes that there's a big difference between your OKR management system and your transaction and data source systems. So, KPIs should not be automatically updated; the hunt for the correct number, consideration of progress, and plan for the future are vital aspects of a successful OKR program.

The other school of thought is to integrate heavily. With this school of thought, the mantra is, "I would like to set up my Objectives and Key Results, but then update the key result from different sources of transaction systems that I normally use to run my business."

Manual check-ins

OKR tracking is completely independent of business transactions

Automated check-ins

OKR tracking is completely integrated with business transactions

Figure 5.2: This spectrum represents the two schools of thought companies take in regard to automating check-ins. On the left, there's the belief that check-ins should never be automated, and on the right, that as many as possible can be automated.

So, which school of thought is "better"?

As always, the answer to this question is the universal management answer, which is: it depends.

As this book has already discussed in detail, your company's OKR program is uniquely tailored to your business's structure, process, and culture.

So, it's truly up to you. What makes sense for your OKR program, its goals, and the processes you are using to see the best results? Should you integrate completely, or let the OKR check-in process unfold without any automation?

This is a choice you will have to figure out through trial and error. You can start out on one end of the spectrum, and slowly adjust based on feedback from your team, how your review meetings are going, and what your business is getting out of your OKR program.

Organizational Philosophy

As you know, OKRs need to be at the top of your mind at all times throughout the quarter. The importance of this part of the OKR framework can be reinforced by encouraging your employees to update their KPI progress themselves.

There is a small amount of additional effort, but the organization feels that it is worth it. Many large businesses practicing OKRs, including Google, do not integrate transaction systems with their OKR tracking.

Many companies might say, "*for an individual who's working on a few KRs, the goals are in their heads all the time.*" And therefore ask, "*why do you even have to go and look for the value?*".

Most of the time, if it is a relatively stable KPI, you'll have the value in your head. If not, you may have to look into your transaction system to get the latest number. But the idea is if you have that kind of a philosophical boundary, then it is no problem. You do not have to do any integrations.

If you think that it is a waste of time to update KPI values manually, you are not necessarily wrong. It is not a bad idea to put some integrations in place so that data flows into your spreadsheets or to your OKR tracking application. You get the benefit of boosting productivity, saving time, and increasing accuracy.

Check-in Meeting Preparedness

If you decide to automate, you should ensure that individuals are still sharing their confidence level and comments on their key result check-ins. You don't want people coming to meetings unprepared, which tends to happen with automation.

Often, especially in the initial days when employees are still figuring the OKR process out, they may arrive at the meeting with their updated KPI in hand, but no plan for making progress.

That is a red flag. Managers should encourage employees to write their analyses by answering questions such as:

- What worked?

- What did not work?

- How do they feel about the rest of the quarter?

- How are they planning to achieve the remaining portion of the KR?

- What other important information did you learn or reflect on this week?

This analysis results in some level of reflection and conversations with other people who will help the key result owner review, comment, and plan for the next few weeks of the quarter. That is all valuable, and conversation is critical to OKR success. Automatic updates can often result in inadequate analyses.

If there is little to no commentary, then your employees can't strike up conversations about key result progress. The check-in process is a little bit like a chain reaction; you have to get through one aspect of the process in order to reap the benefits of the other.

Final Thoughts

So, the question is: should you integrate and automate updates to KPI values in your key results?

A good balance of the two schools of thought explained above is to take a conservative approach to automation, but do not discount automation entirely. At the start of your OKR journey, it's best to keep employees in the thick of their key results. Do not place too much emphasis on automation right from the get-go.

While always having the right key result value on hand can be incredibly useful, ensure any automation is balanced out by proper commentary and reflection. Automating KPI updates does not guarantee your OKR program's success, but inaccurate data will be of no help to anyone. You should selectively integrate KPIs and automate check-ins. Additionally, always pay attention to the status and comments that accompany automated check-ins so that all updates are still informative and beneficial for your OKR program.

6

Why do you see Unbalanced Progress in your OKRs?

If you have been researching the OKR framework, you may have heard that the ideal number of objectives and their corresponding key results is between three and five: 3-5 objectives, and 3-5 key results per objective. You could call this the rule of five, since many agree that this is the sweet spot for OKRs.

However, you might find yourself asking: why is this the case?

At every level of a business you set OKRs— corporate, departmental, cross-functional team and individual—the rule of 5 holds true. Let's take a closer look at why setting 3-5 OKRs is the right choice across all levels of your organization.

Why Do I Need 3-5 OKRs?

The simple answer to this question is "focus". Focus is one of the key tenets of the OKR methodology.

By dedicating your focus to three to five objectives, and limiting the number of key results per

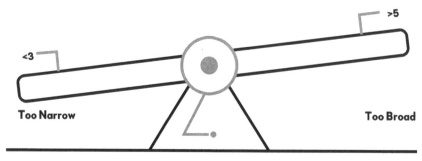

Figure 6.1: If you have less than three objectives per level, or key results per objective, your focus is too narrow, and chances are you will have extra bandwidth and more room for improvement. Meanwhile, if you have more than five objectives per level or key results per objective, you're stretching yourself too thin and will end up focusing on too many things at once.

objective to this range as well, the OKR framework offers a reasonable list to operate with.

If you have more than five OKRs, it can work against you in major ways. A lack of focus has the potential to stall progress and limit success in your business. If you have less than three OKRs, though, you've narrowed down your line of sight so much that any progress you make will be one-dimensional. While limiting the scope of OKRs can be beneficial, going too narrow may not be appropriate or useful for your business.

The rule of five isn't necessarily a hard and fast rule– it's more of a guideline. However, OKR champions all agree that this bracket will help you and your team focus, while also helping you drive productivity in multiple areas, meaning you're making multi-dimensional progress that has a real impact in your business.

All businesses that implement an OKR program usually have the same end result in mind: achieving their goals and helping their company succeed. To determine if this end result is met, many people undergo the reflect and reset process at the end of the quarter. While this process is useful, it's not the only way that businesses can see OKR progress.

There are visible signs that can help you determine if your OKR program is working correctly at any point throughout the quarter. One of these signs is balanced progress between OKRs.

Balanced progress in your OKR program means that all company OKRs are progressing at an equal pace. This reflects how well your team is performing across the board. Comparing actual progress to planned progress is useful in determining how effective your planning was, as well as how effective your execution is.

A Closer Look

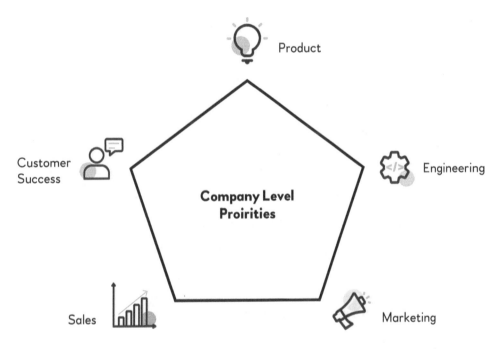

Figure 6.2: Five priority departments that might appear at the company level of your OKR program.

Let's look at an example.

At the company level, you might have a balanced plan that consists of five well-developed OKRs. Each one focuses on a different aspect of the business: product, engineering, marketing, sales, and customer success.

An OKR champion can tell you that the key to a healthy OKR program is frequent check-ins and meetings. When discussing the progress of each of your five company-level OKRs mid-quarter, planned progress might be at 40%, while actual progress is also at 40%. Alternatively, maybe one OKR has exceeded progress– reaching 50%-60% completion while planned progress is 40%. Meanwhile, another OKR's progress could be lagging behind the planned progress mark at 20%.

Even though one OKR is progressing ahead of schedule, this isn't a good sign for your OKR program. This unequal progress demonstrates an imbalance between departments, and can point to larger issues within the organization. Taking a closer look at the sub-functions of departments might reveal that there are key problems within your organization that need to be resolved. If progress on OKRs is not balanced across the board, there could be issues that have to do with resource allocation, focus, or even talent.

If progress is lagging behind in one department or on one OKR, you should examine the specific department or team responsible and its sub-functions. For example, if your OKR focused on marketing isn't meeting planned targets, take a look at all the components of that department. Are there issues within event marketing? Inbound marketing via content? Outbound marketing? Email messaging? Try to get to the root cause of the issue.

When you identify the key problem areas within your organization, you need to address them. These lower-level problems can greatly impact the progress of higher-level OKRs. Ensuring that you dedicate time and attention to these problem areas might seem time-consuming, however these issues have the potential to derail your goals, making it vitally important that you address issues where you see them– even if they seem to be lower-order concerns.

What are the causes of Balanced OKR Progress?

If you have set your OKRs using the best practices outlined in this OKR program series and are monitoring progress, you may find that all OKRs are progressing as planned. This means that none are pulling ahead over the others, or lagging behind.

There are a few reasons this might be happening, and it's important to meditate on these reasons so that you can try to replicate this success in other departments, or in future quarters. Take some time during the learning stage of your PEEL cycle to reflect on what went right. Here are some examples of what that might look like:

1. Even Talent Distribution

Not every member of your company's team will have the same talents; that's why it's important for managers to recognize every individual's strengths and ensure that team members have complementary talents as they work towards common goals.

If you see balanced progress across your OKRs, it might be a good indicator that team members are working well together, and all individual talents are being put to good use.

2. Well-Developed OKRs

Sometimes, as companies set OKRs and determine their quarterly targets, they can turn stretch goals– which are encouraged– into downright unrealistic goals that employees can't possibly achieve. When this happens, targets tend to demoralize employees rather than motivate them.

However, if your actual progress correlates with your planned progress, this is a good indicator that you have read the capabilities of your company, department, or team correctly. This signals that your goals are realistic, and you have clear objectives, and substantive key results. This could be the result of a mature OKR program, or simply a well-developed set of OKRs.

3. Committed Employees

If your OKR progress is balanced, it could be an indicator that your team is committed to their assigned goals. The OKR framework requires users to demonstrate dedication and attention to the various processes that go into tracking and progressing OKRs.

If employees are committed, this means that they are prioritizing their OKRs over other projects, are checking in on a weekly basis, and are also utilizing weekly PPP meetings to get the help they need and move the needle on their important goals. This commitment translates to well-balanced OKRs, and indicates that the learning culture necessary for OKR execution is well-integrated into your company. Balanced OKR progress suggests you have employees that understand the OKR methodology and its benefits, and are doing all they can to reach even the most ambitious goals.

16 Reasons your OKR Progress is Unbalanced

Even when you take all the right steps to roll out your OKR program, there are times when issues might still come up. It could be the case that you have five OKRs, and you're making steady progress on two of them– but three are stuck.

Efficiency is doing better what is already being done.

Peter Drucker

If you're facing unbalanced progress in your OKR program, there are four key areas you need to look at to find out if something is going wrong: Leader, Team, Target, or Review Process. Issues can arise in any one of these areas that cause unbalanced progress. Let's take a closer look at these specific areas.

Figure 6.3: Sixteen possible reasons behind your unbalanced OKR progress. Usually, the culprit lies in one of these four categories: the leader, the review process, the team, or the target.

Leader

1. Shifts Focus Often

The first potential source of your OKR program's unbalanced progress could be the program's leader.

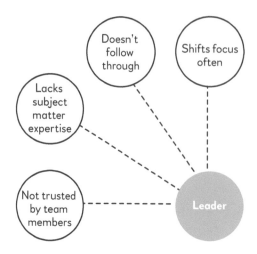

When it comes to examining the leader, it's important to see if they have a focus issue. If the leader is setting priorities but shifting the team's focus, it can be difficult for individuals to make substantial progress on the key results that must be achieved. Multiple studies have shown that issues with leadership and issues with focus go hand-in-hand.

When there's a problem with focus, many important tasks and initiatives are started, but few are finished. Jumping from one task to the next keeps a team busy adjusting their priorities, but leaves a wake of unfinished work and a low output behind.

2. Doesn't Follow Through

The second leader-centric issue that your OKR problem could be facing is a leader that doesn't follow through.

This is similar to the first issue, focus, but boils down to a lack of persistence and ability to see projects through to the end. If a leader can't drive productivity on important tasks and projects, then key targets will not be fulfilled, leading to unbalanced progress in an OKR program.

3. Lacks Subject Matter Expertise

It could be that the leader of a certain team lacks the vital skills necessary to manage and lead projects in their area.

If the leader of the engineering team isn't well-versed in engineering principles, has never managed engineering projects, or isn't up to speed on the technological and functional knowledge needed to lead the team, this could be a major issue causing some OKRs to lag behind others.

4. Not Trusted by Their Team

There could be a variety of reasons that team members don't trust in their leader. This could be due to a lack of knowledge surrounding subject matter, or simply a lack of confidence in communicating with the team.

Whatever the cause, the bottom line is that the team doesn't believe that they have the support they need to drive a project forward and see it through to the end. A team's lack of trust in their leader can slow down projects and stall progress on important OKRs.

Team

The next potential problem area you should examine if you're facing unbalanced progress is the team.

1. Lacks Subject Matter Expertise

Like the leader, a team itself could lack familiarity or expertise in their department's subject matter. A lack of expertise can stunt the capability of a team as a whole.

This problem can be solved by getting the right people to perform the right tasks. For example, if you're managing the sales team and see a gap in capability and expertise, you need to hire

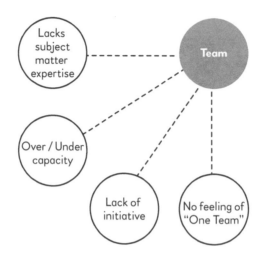

someone skilled in that area. If you lack a sales process, you should onboard someone who excels at creating and executing processes to guide the team and teach this skill. If you have the wrong people with experience that doesn't match the needs of your team, there will be too much trial and error to make substantial progress on your OKRs.

2. Over Capacity or Under Capacity

There are a few issues that can arise related to team capacity. First, over capacity is a problem if a team can blaze through a few initiatives with ease. While this might sound like a good thing, it's actually an indication that you have too many team members committed to projects that simply don't require those resources.

This issue might be paired with the second capacity-related issue– under capacity. If you have too many people committed to one project, and too few on another, teams will underachieve, not reaching their full potential or making the progress they need to in order to fulfill priorities.

3. Lack of Initiative

Third, a team might lack initiative and drive. When team members lack initiative, projects stall simply because people are waiting for things to fall into place, or for the next task in the pipeline to move without following up with the individuals responsible for the task.

If no one is there to take the initiative and answer the important questions needed in order for a project to move forward, then things can stall indefinitely. This might come down to an individual capability or attitude problem, or a team could simply have a bad combination of problems. This issue has the potential to impact team progress in a big way, and could be the piece of the puzzle that isn't falling into place when it comes to OKR progress.

4. No Feeling of "One Team"

If individuals on a team don't have a sense of camaraderie and common goals to unite them, this can spark many issues. The feeling that not everyone is on the same team could be centralized in a certain department, or it could be a broader cultural issue within a company.

The side effects of this can include many arguments and disagreements, and an unwillingness for individuals to help other departments or coworkers. If collaboration is a chore rather than a natural element of a team's or a company's dynamic, the business can suffer. There must be a feeling of unification under the same goals.

Otherwise, situations might arise where teams fall out of alignment with other departments, or in and of themselves. For example, the swift implementation of new features by the engineering team doesn't spell success for the company if they don't address the concerns that customer success raises from customers. Prioritizing a feeling of unity and being on the same team can help balance progress in your organization.

Target

The third area that you need to examine if you're facing unbalanced progress with your OKRs is the target itself.

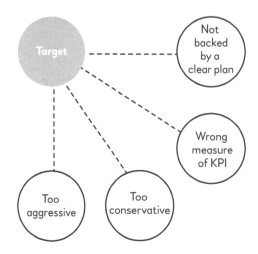

1. Too Aggressive

First, the target for an OKR that is lagging behind might be more aggressive than the other OKR targets. This isn't necessarily an issue that stands on it's own. It's possible that leader- and team-related issues could contribute to issues with your target. A lack of communication between a leader and their team, for example, might have caused an OKR to be set at a target that surpasses "ambitious" and becomes "unachievable".

2. Too Conservative

Alternatively, unbalanced progress could be due to a disproportionately conservative target. If a target isn't ambitious and pushing the limit, a team might end up achieving and surpassing the target for a key result or objective.

Similar to the "too aggressive" issue, this problem might arise from a combination of other problems regarding communication or trust between team members and leadership. Additionally, it could be an attitude issue within the team called "sandbagging", where individuals purposefully set their target too low to ensure they achieve it.

3. Wrong Measurement of KPI

This is an interesting issue to consider if you are facing unbalanced progress and can't get a sense of why an OKR is lagging behind. Trying to track an OKR using the wrong measurement or KPI is like trying to climb up one ladder while you're standing on another.

This might stem from an issue with alignment, or even an understanding of all the tools that are at your disposal for a certain initiative. If you're trying to measure a key result with a KPI that doesn't match, you naturally won't see progress- or, alternatively, you'll see progress that doesn't actually reflect the true state of a key result.

If you're completing an initiative to increase customer satisfaction, but trying to measure it using a sales or marketing metric, you're not going to be able to track the impact your projects are having.

4. Not Backed by a Clear Plan

The fourth issue you might find when examining your targets is that they are not backed by a clear plan. If you set a target and create a list of planned activities that does not follow the MECE principle- of being mutually exclusive and collectively exhaustive- then you won't be able to reach your target.

Without a clearly-defined plan laid out to help guide your team to impact set targets, you will see unbalanced progress.

Review Process

The fourth area that you need to take a hard look at if you want to find the source of your unbalanced OKR progress is the review process.

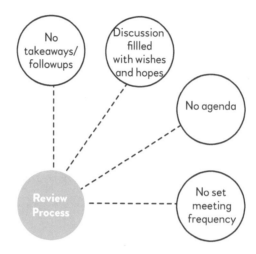

1. No Set Meeting Frequency

In order to successfully stay aligned and follow through on priorities, there needs to be a set meeting frequency. Having meetings localized at different levels at the organization or on a case-by-case basis leaves individuals with no agenda, organization, or ability to anticipate when they can coordinate with their team members.

Having a dedicated meeting such as a PPP meeting to review progress, plans, and problems helps teams check in with one another on a regular basis. This allows for teams to check the pulse on priorities, collaborate on issues, and get a sense of how everyone in the organization is doing on their goals. If a meeting like this doesn't exist, there is a major disconnect that can cause a variety of issues– including an imbalance of OKR progress.

2. No Agenda

Let's say that you have a meeting with a set frequency. This gives you the opportunity to coordinate with other individuals. But what if there's no set agenda?

A meeting without a clearly-managed agenda means that important time is wasted, and projects and other important tasks can begin to slip through the cracks. Meetings are useful when there's a clear record of everything discussed previously, and the items that overflowed from one week to the next. Without an agenda, individuals might not bring their important questions to the table, and this could cause progress to slow and stall out.

3. Discussion Filled with Wishes & Hopes

Process issues breed more process issues. A lack of a clear agency and direction for a discussion can lead you to issue number three– an unproductive, useless discussion filled with wishes and hopes rather than concrete plans and action items.

Structuring discussion in meetings is vitally important so that everyone has the opportunity to present what they have completed, the results of their progress, the methods that worked out, and the strategies that were not useful. Not having that structure means that discussion is aimless and based on a hazy outline of what is happening in the company rather than the concrete data and information available.

4. No Takeaways / No Follow-Ups

Ineffective meetings and discussions can leave important items vague, and give team members a sense that things will simply get sorted out as they go along. This mindset, combined with poor review processes, gives individuals no takeaways from meetings, and does not encourage people to follow up on assigned tasks.

If individuals don't leave meetings with clear action items, deadlines, or concrete tasks to complete, then what was the point of the meeting itself? Running review processes in this way is simply a disaster waiting to happen– and that can culminate in the form of unbalanced progress on your OKRs.

Solving Unbalanced Progress at the Corporate Level

Knowing the potential reasons behind unbalanced progress can be helpful when identifying issues that are holding your business back.

> *Teamwork is the ability to work together toward a common vision. The ability to direct individual accomplishments toward organizational objectives. It is the fuel that allows common people to attain uncommon results.*

 Andrew Carnegie

Let's take a look at a framework to analyze situations that exhibit unbalanced progress, using the potential causes discussed above.

In the following example, a few potential problems have been flagged for a given situation. While there could be a myriad of issues lurking beneath unbalanced progress, and you should always investigate the red flags you see, you can use this case study as a starting point to understand how these issues can play out.

Unbalanced Progress: Team and Target

In this example, there is unbalanced progress on a 5-OKR radar chart for a company's corporate-level OKRs. These are the top priorities for a company in the given quarter.

This meets the rule of 5 for OKRs, however progress is wildly unbalanced. If the blue line within the pentagon represents planned progress, and the orange shape represents actual progress, then there's a clear imbalance among these five OKRs. Let's take a closer look.

1. Over/Under Capacity

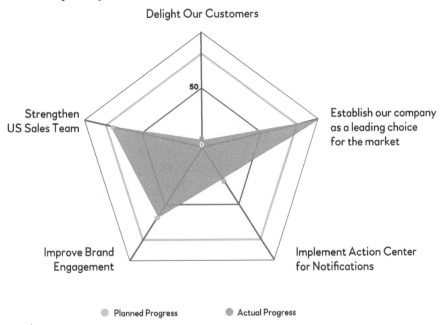

The second OKR at this level is "Establish our company as a leading choice for the market". This OKR has already been completed, even though there are a few weeks left in the quarter. When contrasted against OKRs such as the first one, "Delight Our Customers," you might notice that something isn't quite right.

The problem could be with over or under capacity. With "Establish our company as a leading choice for the market," it seems that the team blazed through the OKR with ease. While this could be a good thing, it might be a signal that the company overcommitted resources and team members for the success of this objective. The excess team members could have been helping out with initiatives that were lagging behind, and wasted resources are an issue that can snowball in no time.

Meanwhile, the initiative for "Delight Our Customers" fell completely behind. In the effort to become a leader in the market with outbound initiatives, the team didn't commit to the customers they already had, leaving the resources for this goal at under capacity and allowing progress to fall behind.

2. Not Backed by a Clear Plan

The next problem could come in the form of target issues. Take a look at the OKR to "Implement an Action Center for Notifications". This is an objective that would require key results that follow the MECE principle of being mutually exclusive and collectively exhaustive. If this objective isn't backed by a clearly-defined plan that covers all the necessary aspects of rolling out an action center for notifications, then the objective simply will not be fulfilled.

This is a problem that dates back to the planning stage of the OKR cycle. Before this OKR even began making progress, it was doomed to fail. Ensure you have all the tools you need to write amazing OKRs, and dedicate more time and care to planning out your OKRs in the next quarter.

3. Too Aggressive

The last potential reason behind this radar chart's unbalanced progress is another issue related to targets. While OKRs encourage you to be ambitious and reach for the stars, leaders need to work with their team to come up with a target number that is a stretch, but not an impossibility.

As you can see with the fourth OKR on this chart, "Improve Brand Engagement," progress is moving, but it is still failing to meet expectations. This is an issue that also begins at the Planning stage of the PEEL cycle– but it also is one that seemingly went unnoticed throughout the entire quarter.

In order to have the most success with OKRs, you need to commit to weekly or biweekly meetings to check in on team progress. This is a designated time where teams can touch base on progress, problems, and plans, and make a game plan to get back on track if they have strayed off course.

Solving Unbalanced Progress: Marketing Department Imbalance

At times, your radar chart doesn't indicate you're progressing as you might have hoped. Instead, it might present unbalanced progress on your OKRs. While this gives you a great idea of which OKRs are lagging behind and signals that you should re-commit to those OKRs, there might be even more information to derive from this scenario.

There are a myriad of potential reasons that you might be facing unbalanced OKRs in your organization.

Coming together is a beginning, staying together is progress, and working together is success.

Henry Ford

Let's take a look at some potential ways that unbalanced OKR progress might play out in real life with the radar chart below.

This radar chart indicates that there are six OKRs for the Marketing Department. As you can see, three of these OKRs are progressing either on track, or are exceeding expected progress. The other three OKRs are lagging behind. While it's possible to recommit and catch up on

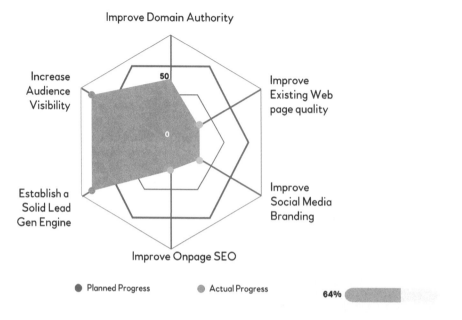

progress, it's important that you analyze the cause of this imbalance, and attempt to correct it from the source so that your future OKRs are stronger.

The very first issue with the goals on this OKR level should be obvious– they did not follow the rule of five that dictates that each level should have between three and five OKRs.

Outside of that issue, however, there is still drastically unbalanced progress on this radar chart. Let's take a look at the potential reasons behind this imbalance.

Unbalanced Progress: Leader, Team, Target, & Process

1. The Leader Doesn't Follow Through

If a team is led by a leader that doesn't follow through on projects or have the persistence to drive productivity, OKR progress could look something like the third OKR in the above example, "Improve Social Media Branding".

As you can see, progress is not at zero– there has been some movement on this OKR. However, it seems to have stalled out at the halfway point. It could be that the progress made was a collection of smaller tasks and projects that did not deviate too far from the regular day-to-day responsibilities of the team members working on the OKR.

However, there was no follow up from the leader, or a push to do more. Now, a few weeks from the end of the quarter, progress is leagues behind where it should be, and the OKR will most likely not even reach the 70% threshold expected of a stretch OKR.

2. Over Capacity/Under Capacity

An issue with over or under capacity could also be the reason behind the imbalanced progress seen on this radar chart. These six OKRs for the marketing department should be split among the team in such a way that allows every initiative to have the resources and people it needs to succeed.

That is not happening on this radar chart. For the OKR to "Establish a Solid Lead Gen Engine," a lot of people were dedicated to this job. Maybe the team produced ebooks for their lead-gen engine, and committed time, effort, and resources to getting this done. While this is a vital OKR to make progress on, the team is significantly overshooting the expected progress.

Meanwhile, the OKR to "Improve Onpage SEO" is severely lagging behind expected progress. While a large group of department members and department time has been dedicated to establishing a lead gen engine, the onpage SEO initiative has been left in the dust, perhaps left in the hands of only one or two people, when it was meant to be a team effort.

3. Too Aggressive

What happens when a target surpasses "ambitious" and becomes "unachievable"?

It will probably have the look of the third OKR on this radar chart- "Improve Social Media Branding".

This issue has everything to do with team communication and the planning stage of the PEEL cycle for OKRs— where companies plan, execute, engage, and learn during their OKR program. During the planning phase of the PEEL cycle, teams and leaders should communicate their priorities for the quarter, the bandwidth of the team, and what everyone wants to achieve. OKRs should contribute to overall company goals and priorities, however it's still important to take stock of what is possible, and find a target that's past a safe bet, but not completely impossible with the resources and constraints of the department.

For "Improve Social Media Branding," it could be the case that the key result targets for setting up new social media presences, engaging and growing followers, and collaborating with important thought influencers in your field were set too high. You might have achieved a great deal– but your radar chart will show little to no progress.

This isn't an accurate reflection of the department's progress. When something that seemed feasible and straightforward isn't progressing as expected, it's important to take a closer look at the way key results have been formulated, and what progress has been made so far.

4. No Set Meeting Frequency

When it comes to OKRs, touching base with your team is incredibly important. If you don't have a great line of communication open, you might see situations similar to the second example OKR above– "Improving Existing Webpage Quality". This OKR made some progress, but has stalled completely, lagging so far behind expectations that catching up will be incredibly difficult. What went wrong here?

First, if there's no consistent meeting frequency in your department, you might see an OKR like this one. This department has six important OKRs to look after. If team members don't know what to do on one of their priorities, chances are they will move on to another and make an impact where they can.

Worse, if there's no set meeting frequency, there's no space to follow up on this. So, individuals might explain in their check-ins that they're stuck, but if there's no follow up, or meeting to coordinate with team members and make a game plan for progress, then there simply won't be any movement on this initiative.

5. No Agenda

Let's say you do have weekly meetings. This doesn't necessarily mean the problem will be fixed. Even with weekly team sync-ups, you might still see OKRs with progress like "Improve Existing Webpage Quality". Why?

It could be because your meeting, even though it is scheduled, doesn't have a set agenda. The team might be so busy discussing what progress was made and explaining day-to-day issues that they forget to touch base about the OKR that no one has been able to make progress on.

Many OKR experts recommend following the PPP meeting method, or something similar. This gives a structure to meetings; here, you first touch on the progress that has been made, then the plans you have moving forward, and finally the problems that came up in the past week. This gives teams a framework to cover all the topics that need to be discussed within the meeting time, so nothing gets left behind, and important OKRs don't go untouched for weeks on end.

Solving Unbalanced Progress: Sales Department Imbalance

Even when you do everything right when setting your OKRs and getting started with your OKR quarter, you can still face issues with progress.

When your OKR progress within a department or team is unbalanced, it's a sign that there's something amiss in one of four areas– the Leadership, the Team, the Target, or the Processes behind OKR progress.

Unbalanced Progress: Leader, Team, Target, and Process

Below, we'll explore a case study of unbalanced progress. Here, there's a sales department's five OKRs for quarter three, which is just a few weeks away from ending, as signified by the black outline. This represents where progress should be at this point in the quarter, which would place all OKRs on track to be completed by the end of the quarter.

Effectively, change is almost impossible without industry-wide collaboration, cooperation, and consensus.

Simon Mainwaring
CEO of We First, Inc.,

As you can see by the orange shaded OKR progress area, OKR progress isn't on track.

Why the imbalance? Let's break down how the potential reasons for unbalanced OKR progress are making an appearance on the Sales department's radar chart.

1. Discussion Filled with Wishes & Hopes

Process issues are incredibly impactful and harmful when it comes to making consistent and proper progress on your OKRs. For the second OKR on this radar chart, "Establish Active Reseller's Channel," the sales team may have set up concrete key results revolving around demos and deals. However, even though these tangible key results and associated KPIs are in place, the sales team is still falling short.

This might come down to the discussion that department members are engaging in during

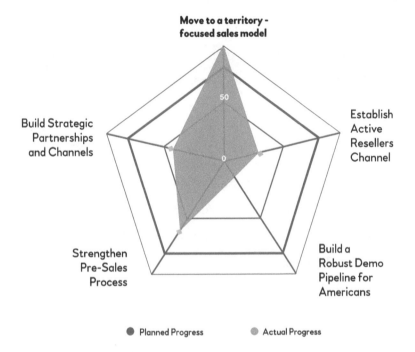

meetings regarding this OKR. Even if a meeting is on the schedule and an agenda is in place, the discussion might lack agency and direction. Instead, the sales department could be talking less about tangible KPIs and more about wishes and hopes. These conversations are useless without concrete action items. If there is no task to complete, there is no movement on a key result, leading to a lack of progress on the OKR as a whole.

2. No Takeaways/No Follow-Ups

A process issue like insubstantial discussions can lead to further issues. If the sales department isn't having good discussions, there's very little chance that team members can take away anything useful from the meeting itself. Because of this, there's very little for peers and leaders to follow up on.

Instead, meetings need to be filled with action items, deadlines, or tasks. Otherwise, the OKR will stall, as seen with "Establish Active Reseller's Channel" on the radar chart.

3. Too Conservative

Let's take a look at the first OKR on this radar chart, "Move to a territory-focused sales model". The progress for this OKR is complete. When progress is unbalanced like this, and there is one OKR leagues ahead of others, it's important to take a close look at the outlier.

With this OKR, you might find that it has been complete for weeks. Why is this the case?

It could be that the targets associated with this OKR were too conservative. With this example to change the sales model, it's possible that the Sales department ran into an issue with sandbagging. Sandbagging is when individuals set their targets low so that they will undoubtedly achieve them. This makes them look better, and makes it appear as though they are excelling at achieving their OKRs.

When this happens, take a close look at the OKR. In this case, if the key results revolved around generating new leads, or creating new sales territory business plans, were they ambitious enough? Does the completion of the key results truly set the sales team up for success next quarter, when they begin selling in these territories?

This is an important habit for leaders to catch onto, and an even more important one to break within a department. While sandbagging might help a department look good at the end-of-quarter meeting, it certainly won't turn out well in the long run, when they're not well-prepared for what lies ahead. It's also important to note that OKRs should not be tied directly to performance reviews, promotions, or pay raises– this gives team members reason to set the bar low and achieve high.

4. Lacks Subject Matter Expertise

Take a look at the fifth OKR in this case study example; "Establish Strategic Partnerships and Channels". This OKR has made some progress, but lags behind planned progress.

If the leader of this OKR is someone who lacks expertise in establishing partnerships, the OKR progress might look something like this. Partnering in business is incredibly important, and it isn't necessarily easy. Establishing positive relationships with other sellers and solidifying that partnership isn't a natural-born skill, and if the individual responsible for doing this isn't experienced, efforts can fall flat time and time again.

When OKRs like this lag behind, it's good practice to look into the individuals responsible for each key result. Are the assignees fit for the job? What is their background with this specific skill? When leadership asks these questions early on, they can assign another, more experienced individual to the key results and create a learning opportunity for the inexperienced individual, as well as maintain progress on important initiatives.

5. Not Trusted by Their Team

When OKRs are "In Trouble," there is usually a strong reason behind it.

One that many leaders might not think of is the relationship between leadership and the team members responsible for an OKR. The third OKR in this case study, "Build a Robust Demo Pipeline for the Americas" might be paired with concrete key results, however progress is still not moving.

This might be due to a lack of trust in the leadership. This could happen for a number of reasons– it could be that the leader has a lack of confidence when communicating with the team, they lack knowledge in how to drive this OKR, or they don't follow through on projects when the team needs them to.

If the team feels that they don't have the support they need to drive an OKR, progress can stall. Establishing a demo pipeline can involve many moving parts and can be a large time commitment for individuals. If they feel their team leader won't listen to them when they explain their bandwidth, or will not provide the right resources to help them achieve, they might not even be motivated to budge this OKR any more than they can with day-to-day activities.

7

What is Organizational Learning and why is it important?

"In less than 15 years, one third of the fortune 500 companies have disappeared, and the average lifetime for the largest enterprises is less than 40 years." This was a shocking observation by Peter M Senge, the MIT Professor who coined the term "Learning Organization". He was named as "strategist of the century" by the Journal of Business Strategy.

So how can companies that excelled and climbed their way to the top suddenly plunge? And how do other companies manage to stay consistently at the top?

> **Leadership and learning are indispensable to each other**

 John F. Kennedy

The secret is that companies that stay on top have committed to a Learning Organization model. According to Peter Senge, a learning organization is a group of people working together collectively to enhance their capacities to create results they really care about.

The Five Elements of a Learning Organization:

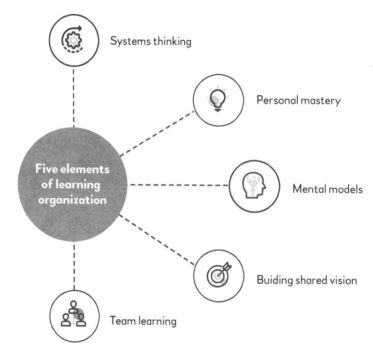

Figure 7.1: *This infographic displays the 5 key elements of a learning organization.*

1. Systems Thinking

Systems thinking is about thinking and visualizing the system as a whole instead of focusing on individual issues. You can also call this element "the ability to see the big picture".

In many cases, the correlation between action and consequences may occur in different periods. For example, if a company decides to cut its R&D budget, it may increase its profit in the short term, but it could be causing irreparable harm to the competitiveness of the firm in the long run.

2. Personal Mastery

Peter M. Senge refers to *Personal Mastery* as an approach towards a skill or craft similar to how a master artist approaches their art. People pursuing personal mastery of a certain skill are committed to *lifelong learning* and work to achieve results that designate them as the best in their field.

An organization's learning *"capacity and commitment"* cannot be greater than its members. Therefore, the connection between *"Personal learning"* and *"Organizational learning"* is vital.

Organizations need to create a culture that values *Personal Mastery* and provides tools that enable employees to hone their craft— no matter what industry or sector of the business those employees are in.

3. Mental Models

According to Peter M. Senge, *mental models* are deeply ingrained assumptions and generalizations that influence how people understand the world and how they act. People are often not consciously aware of their mental models or the effects they have on their behaviour.

For example, you may observe a quiet person who seldom talks in meetings and say to yourself that this person does not seem to understand what is being discussed.

On the other hand, you might assume that someone who forcefully makes her points in meetings wants to dominate the discussion. Mental models of what can or cannot be done in different management settings can also be deeply entrenched. Many new insights are brushed aside as they may conflict with powerful, existing mental models.

Both of the assumptions about the above people might be incorrect. The quiet person could simply be more comfortable expressing their contributions in writing rather than verbally, meanwhile the conversationalist could actually be offering opinions in order to gain a better understanding of the topic at hand.

This crops up in markets as well. An executive failing to allocate resources to attractive markets could have a mental model that *"Emerging markets are difficult to crack"*. In reality, that executive could just fail to allocate resources early enough, and simply be losing to competition.

4. Building Shared Vision

One of the key qualities of leadership is the ability to create a shared vision for the organization, i.e., a shared picture of the future that the organization will create.

For example, Tesla's vision is "To accelerate the world's transition to sustainable energy". LinkedIn's vision is "To connect the world's professionals to make them more productive and successful." Amazon's vision is "To be Earth's most customer-centric company."

Converting the *personal vision* of a leader to the *shared vision* of an organization is a crucial challenge, and one that organizations must find a way to achieve if they want to excel.

5. Team Learning

In sports, business, sciences, and other aspects of life, we have seen teams without a complete roster of star players excel through coordinated action.

The San Antonio Spurs in the NBA is a good example. Peter M. Senge also observes that teams, when genuinely learning, produce extraordinary results, enabling an individual's rapid growth and development.

When people join the workforce right after college, most enter with great enthusiasm looking forward to a lifetime of learning and working with a purpose. And yet, few organizations have a culture that encourages risk-taking, experimentation, continuous learning, and tolerance for failure.

Live as if you were to die tomorrow. Learn as if you were to live forever.

Mahatma Gandhi

But with rapid changes in the business world such as ubiquitous broadband, digitization, and changing customer preferences, the organizations that do not institutionalize learning can quickly lose ground and become obsolete.

It is predominantly because they will lack the agility required to respond to changes unleashed by the changing business environment, or a spirited competitor.

Tell me and I forget, teach me and I may remember, involve me and I learn.

Benjamin Franklin

Culture- The Enabling Factor for Learning

It is the responsibility of the leadership team to create a learning environment.

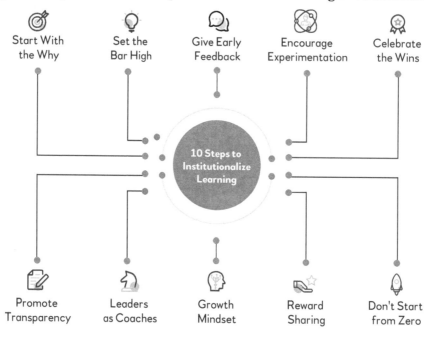

The following are the essential methods to create and nurture a high-performance culture for an outstanding learning environment:

- **Start with the Why:** Leaders should clearly define the Purpose and Mission of the organization. This helps teams to set their learning priorities.

- **Set the Bar High:** Leadership should set the bar high for their teams at every phase of the OKR cycle. Stretch targets help with organizational learning. Additionally, a review of deliverables should reinforce the message of high standards.

- **Give Early Feedback:** Leaders must promote quick, continuous feedback for team members. This improves the agility of an organization and motivates team members to share early and frequently.

- **Encourage experimentation:** Experimentation is the opposite of a business-as-usual mindset and culture. Learning organizations encourage experimentation, tolerate failures, and encourage curiosity.

- **Celebrate the Wins:** Even small wins need to be celebrated. Today's digital organizations usually have tools that encourage collaboration and have internal social networks that can easily recognize great contributors and celebrate victories.

- **Promote Transparency:** All OKRs in an organization should be fully transparent so that the entire company can view everyone's OKRs.

- **Leaders as Coaches:** Leaders should adopt a coach's style by setting ambitious but achievable goals, providing clear and quick feedback, and encouraging team members with their personal and professional development.

- **Growth Mindset:** According to Carol Dweck, who coined the term Growth Mindset, "Individuals who believe their talents can be developed (through hard work, good strategies, and input from others) have a growth mindset. They tend to achieve more than those with a more fixed mindset (those who believe their talents are innate gifts)". This is because individuals with a growth mindset are less worried about looking smart and more worried about learning. When an entire company embraces a growth mindset, their employees report feeling far more empowered and committed.

- **Reward Sharing:** People learn more by teaching. Reward knowledge sharers and discourage hoarders in your company.

- **Do Not Start From Zero:** When organizations institutionalize learning, all employees will gain access to knowledge repositories and can improve their productivity by building on the learning from others. Leadership should avoid *reinventing the wheel* by discouraging people from starting from zero.

The PEEL Methodology – learning in every phase of the OKR lifecycle

Defining a transparent execution methodology like PEEL and baking in Learning as part of the process to execute strategy is a great way to institutionalize learning. To emphasize the importance and effectiveness of this framework, let's take another look at the PEEL Cycle:

Anyone who stops learning is old, whether at twenty or eighty. Anyone who keeps learning stays young.

Henry Ford

Plan:

During the planning stage of the OKR Cycle– usually each quarter– leaders and teams will choose 3 to 5 objectives. This clarifies priorities for the entire organization. If one or more of these priorities concerns learning, this emphasizes to all employees that it should be a part of their daily lives and goals in their work.

Additionally, outlining priorities offers employees clarity on what goals they must focus on. Employees can integrate learning opportunities into these goals as well.

For example, let's say a tech company chooses the Objective *"Improve Sales Efficiency for the quarter"* and the Key Result *"Improve Trial to closure from 10% to 25%"*.

This OKR results in the following learning objectives for the various departments:

- **Sales**– Demo skills, prospecting & closing skills.

- **Marketing**– Generating high-quality leads (trial customers) requires better Digital Marketing skills.

- **Product**– Improving usability and features to accelerate adoption requires better *design* and *engineering skills*.

- **Customer Success**– Improving Customer Engagement requires mapping the customer journey to create a great customer experience.

Thus, OKRs and leadership's learning goals can encourage people by setting ambitious, yet achievable goals.

The Plan phase of the PEEL Cycle is an opportunity for the entire organization to learn the organizations' key focus areas and ensure that the team is clear about overarching goals. It is an achievement by itself for the leadership. Studies have pointed out that up to 95% of the employees in a typical company are not even aware of their organization's strategy.

Execute:

Iterative Business execution is an agile way to experiment with different approaches to solving challenging problems quickly.

Let's go back to a productivity software company's Key Result to "*Improve Trial to Closure from 10% to 25%*". The Product and Customer Experience teams will collaborate and experiment with multiple variations of the product by tweaking the design to help users achieve their goals. The organization can learn by measuring the amount of tasks customers complete, as well as customer engagement with the product.

For example, a SaaS organization might discover that certain personas like CEOs preferred fewer options and a template-based approach that would help them to complete their tasks quickly.

Additionally, a marketing team that experimented with displaying ads in an industry portal targeting sourcing professionals might learn that the click-through rate of their ads is low. Based on this observation, they might tweak their ads, showing the value proposition of their advertised product in numbers instead of catchy slogans, and find that the click through rate improves.

The OKR tool that they used helped them record their lessons learned during their weekly check-ins, and they used intuitive hashtags like #Marketing Lessons— so that even in the future, people can continue to learn from their experiments.

Engage:

The OKR Life Cycle requires teams to do weekly check-ins. The reviews that follow may be great chances for the leadership and team to engage by sharing their approaches and experiments, giving constructive feedback, and even asking for help from other teams.

Many have found that gamification works when it comes to learning. Having reward points for people who contribute to the knowledge repositories and who answer team members' queries can encourage everyone to share more.

Learn:

During the final week of the quarter, the Reflect and Reset process happens. It's a best practice for organizations to have detailed company-wide sessions specifically focused on Lessons Learned during the quarter. Reflecting and resetting helps culminate this learning into a detailed reflection on each OKR.

It is an excellent opportunity for various teams to understand each other's approaches, experiments, achievements, and even failures. Reflections should be stored digitally, or in an easily-accessible location to help companies build a knowledge base of learning.

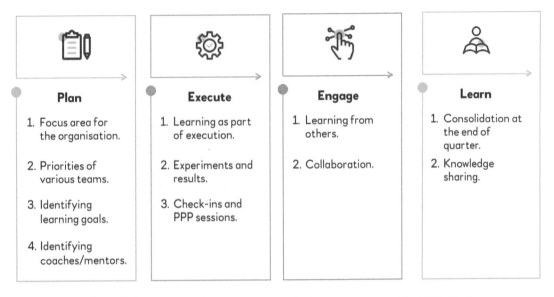

Plan

1. Focus area for the organisation.

2. Priorities of various teams.

3. Identifying learning goals.

4. Identifying coaches/mentors.

Execute

1. Learning as part of execution.

2. Experiments and results.

3. Check-ins and PPP sessions.

Engage

1. Learning from others.

2. Collaboration.

Learn

1. Consolidation at the end of quarter.

2. Knowledge sharing.

Figure 7.2: How organizational learning fits into every stage of the PEEL Cycle.

Tools and Infrastructure for Learning

- **OKR Tools**: A great OKR tool helps teams hardwire learning into their execution processes. They will be able to record their Learning during every phase of the OKR Cycle. Also, it allows them to use hashtags to engage team members and record their lessons learned in the repository.

- **Collaboration Tools**: Collaboration tools like Slack and Microsoft Teams help teams to share their tacit knowledge. Virtual teams require these tools to improve productivity and learn from each other on a daily basis.

- **Knowledge Repository:** Having a useful knowledge repository that can manage unstructured content will be a great asset for building learning organizations. All companies should have a process in place to helps team members easily contribute content, tag information for easy retrieval, and easily search for knowledge.

Tools and Infrastructure for learning

01 **OKR Tool**
Hardwire learning into the team's execution processes.

02 **Collaboration Tool**
Help teams share their tacit knowledge.

03 **Knowledge Repository**
Share knowledge and learnings for everyone to refer to.

04 **Expertise Finder**
Identify experts on the team and connect all employees.

- **Expertise Finder:** Knowledge can be sorted into two categories: Explicit Knowledge and Tacit Knowledge. Explicit Knowledge is information that can be codified and captured in content repositories. Tacit Knowledge is information that is stored in employees' minds, which is implicit and difficult to codify and document. Expert Finder Directories help organizations organize the experts in various skills through directories connected to the collaboration systems, assisting people in searching and finding the right go-to people.

Final Thoughts

In the OKR calendar previously discussed in this book, it is recommended that you dedicate the third Wednesday of each month for brown-bag sessions, and the last Wednesday of the quarter for a town hall session. Both of these sessions celebrate learning throughout the quarter.

But the OKR cycle provides more learning opportunities during weekly PPP reviews to share learning. Ideally, teams should have at least one team huddle to share the learnings each week, right alongside your check-in updates. Remember that the more you learn, the better your OKR program will run, and the more you can achieve. Emphasizing the importance of learning at every opportunity will keep your employees engaged, develop skills and understanding, and spell success for your organization as a whole.

What is organizational learning and why is it important?

8

The quarter is over.
What next?

Setting your OKRs on a quarterly basis gives you a lot of advantages when it comes to continuous improvement. Teams that use the OKR framework have the opportunity to take what they have learned from one quarter— recording what worked, identifying what didn't serve them— and use that knowledge to write stronger OKRs and execute their strategy better in the next quarter.

The process of reflecting on your past quarter and putting those learnings into action is an extremely important pillar of any OKR program. This process is called wrapping your OKR quarter, or reflecting and resetting.

Reflect & Reset

As mentioned in the previous chapter, the Reflect and Reset process is a big opportunity for learning and improvement during your quarter. In the OKR framework, reflecting and resetting is about applying past learnings to future initiatives. Leaders should direct employees to answer a few questions about the success of their OKRs, and take detailed notes on what they believe went well, what didn't, and what needs to change in the future to help the team succeed.

Reflecting and resetting is vitally important for your future success, both with OKRs and as a business. Giving yourself and your team ample time to complete this end-of-quarter process can help you have better outcomes in future quarters.

Steps for Better Reflect & Resets

What can you do to make sure you're getting the most out of your reflect and reset process?

These are the top four steps that you and your team can use to derive the most information and insight out of this process:

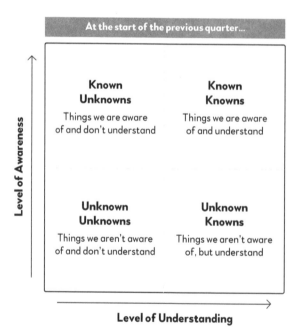

Figure 8.1: The four areas of information in business and a matrix demonstrating a company's awareness and understanding

1. Take Inventory of Your "Known-Knowns"

The first step toward having a better reflect and reset is to take stock of what you know.

Information exists on a matrix of awareness and understanding. First, there are known-knowns— things you are aware of and understand. Then, there are known-unknowns— things you are aware of, but don't understand. Likewise, there are unknown-unknowns— things you aren't aware of, and don't understand. And finally there are unknown-knowns— things you aren't aware of, but understand.

In business, we mostly operate in the known knowns quadrant.

Over the course of a quarter, however, you might have uncovered hidden gems that were previously in the known-unknowns, unknown-knowns, or even the unknown-unknowns category. With new information coming in based on your experiences, those previously unknown things might have migrated to the known-knowns category.

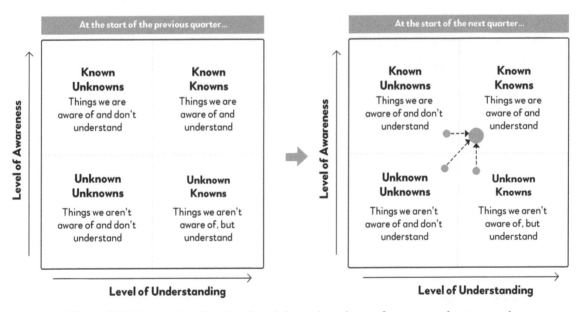

Figure 8.2: Two matrices that show how information migrates from one quadrant to another over the course of a quarter.

For example, you might have had a hunch that partnerships are key to your success. This hunch falls under the unknown-known quadrant. Over the course of the quarter, you might get some concrete signals that confirm your hunch. Now, the notion that "partnerships are key to our success" has moved from being an unknown-known to a known-known. When you establish an organized process around identifying these hidden gems, it is extremely revealing, enlightening, and clarifying.

It is very important to recognize the information that has fallen under things you are aware of and understand. You must take inventory of the known-knowns quadrant at the end of your quarter and evaluate the information you have at your disposal. During your reflect and reset process, you should determine what this new stock of information means for the decisions you make in the upcoming quarter.

Coming up with new initiatives, shutting the door on initiatives that no longer make sense, and ensuring that your chosen key results are creating the best impact on your organization is the best way to make use of this newfound knowledge.

2. Time Travel Back to the Start of Current Quarter

After you have checked your inventory of known-knowns, it's time to do some time-travelling.

Think back to the beginning of your previous quarter, and consider it from the perspective you have now with what you have learned over the quarter. Ask yourself some questions about what you expected from the quarter, and how it ended up, such as:

- What did you plan to accomplish?

- What has changed from the beginning of the quarter to the end of the quarter?

- Do the goals you set for yourself and your team make sense now?

- Did your OKRs have the planned impact you were hoping for?

> › If not, why?

Once you understand these things and have a grasp of what you planned to happen, you can get a better perspective on your execution of the plan, and the actual impact of the accomplishments you fulfilled in that quarter.

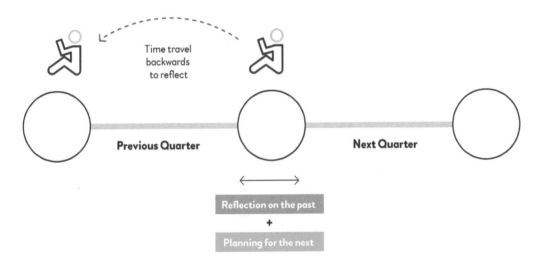

Figure 8.3: *This is a visual representation of how you should "time travel" in order to write reflections that are rich with information and learnings.*

When it comes to work that has not been completed as planned, it is still important to assess the impact during your reflection process. However, you have to answer the critical question: should you continue with that work? Or start something new?

Additionally, there's an even more important question to ask as you time travel back and forth between your perspective at the beginning of a quarter and the end of it. With these perspectives, you should consider if you could have done something that you didn't even consider at the beginning of the quarter. Should you have prioritized one initiative over another? What do you wish you had known?

This information is vital to consider as you reset for your upcoming quarter.

For example, let's say that as you reflect and reset your Q1, you found that you dedicated most of your time to five or six different key results and their corresponding objectives.

However, you remember that, at the beginning of the quarter, you had eight or nine key results that truly felt like top priorities that you planned to get done. How did those fall through the cracks? What could you have done to drive progress on those lagging key results? You may have run out of resources, or simply run out of time, but looking from the perspective of both the end of the quarter, and the beginning, you realize that you would have been in a much better position had you focused more on those key results instead of the ones you actually focused on.

Since you were able to remember why these key results were so important from your perspective at the beginning of the quarter, you can reset your OKRs and make these key results your top priority in Q2. In Q2, you can put in renewed focus, energy, and resources behind completing these important key results.

The reflect and reset process can teach you that key results like these can easily fall through the cracks. Designating them as high-priority, and keeping the issues that caused them to lag behind in mind helps to ensure that your team dedicates proper resources to see them completed.

3. Put Someone Else in Your Shoes

The next step you can take to ensure you're getting the most out of your reflect and reset process is putting yourself in someone else's shoes.

Here, we have a famous example where Andy Grove, the father of OKRs and former CEO & Chairman of Intel, posed a question that would help business leaders for years to come think outside of the box and outside of their own perspective:

> *In the midst of the doldrums of 1985, Grove posed a hypothetical question to his colleague Gordon Moore: "If we got kicked out and the board brought in a new CEO, what do you think he would do?" Moore answered without hesitation, "He would get us out of memories." To which Grove responded, "Why shouldn't you and I walk out the door, come back and do it ourselves?"*
>
> **Harvard Business Review, 1996**

Taking a moment to consider your progress, problems, and plans from a new perspective can change your business for the better. This doesn't have to be between two C-level executives; this can be framed as a group exercise.

How might this exercise look in an example situation?

Let's say you are the head of the marketing department and call a meeting with your direct reports. If you were to tell them to imagine that the CEO decided to replace you, and all your directs, because he feels you need new energy on the team, what would this new team do first?

- Have an open conversation with your team. Ask follow-up questions such as:

  › What would be on top of that new team's list of priorities?

  › What things would they immediately stop doing?

  › What practices would be kept, and what would be discarded for something more efficient?

Trying to identify issues from this perspective can ensure that your team is focusing on the most important things.

This exercise can also be done alone. What would someone new do in your exact position, with the exact issues and resources you have today?

The key to finding valuable insight with this exercise is being open, honest, and making your team comfortable with facing the reality of their situation. Create an environment where people feel safe to identify the real issues, and ensure that people feel the value in this exercise.

While some people might feel that this is a waste of valuable work time, setting the right tone and creating a relaxed atmosphere can encourage people to voice their opinion openly and suggest ideas that they might not feel comfortable voicing in the context of regular work. Carving out space for people to take on a new perspective, and letting yourself critically and objectively examine the state of your initiatives is a great way to ensure you are getting the most out of your reflect and reset process.

4. Time Travel Into the Future to the End of the New Quarter

Finally, once you have your initiatives planned out for the next quarter, it's time to break out the time machine once again. This time, time travel to the end of your next quarter, and try to envision what that might look like after you have accomplished everything you have planned and gained new knowledge.

At the 90-day mark, if you have accomplished the five or ten priorities you've identified for the quarter, will you be happy with your progress? If all goes according to plan, will you be satisfied and be able to say that you have no regrets about what you have dedicated time to, or doubt about the importance of prioritizing these initiatives over others? Can you picture yourself saying "I am happy with my achievements" at next quarter's reflect and reset?

Ask yourself some questions about your state of mind, and the state of your business, if everything goes according to plan:

- Am I happy with the things I have accomplished?

- Do I have any regrets about choosing these things as my priorities?

- Do I wish I could have focused on different initiatives?

  › If so, what are they?

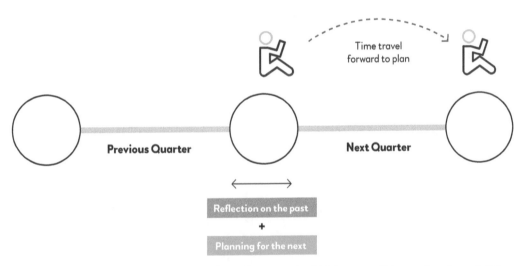

Figure 8.4: This is a visual representation of how you should "time travel" forward to the end of the upcoming quarter when planning your priorities. This exercise helps you determine if your planned OKRs actually address your most important goals and targets.

This exercise acts as a verification process that helps confirm if your plan is the right one. Once creating your strategy for the quarter, it's not wise to simply walk away and see how it works out in 90 days. Instead, you need to think about how you will feel if you execute this strategy perfectly. If there is any trace of doubt or regret, you need to reevaluate and verify your plan with this exercise once again until you know with complete confidence that you will be happy with your achievements.

Weekly or biweekly check-ins grant you the opportunity to ensure that your strategy is going according to plan, however answering these questions can help you perform a higher-level confirmation. This determines if you are committing time, energy, and resources to the right key results, and gives you the chance to change course before you begin.

Final Thoughts

The reflect and reset process at the end of your OKR quarter is the most important thing that you can do to help your business build a stronger and more effective OKR program. Finding ways to derive more value from this process and gather as much insight as possible puts you on the fast track to reaching your goals and honing a more focused and energized team.

9

What red flags should you be on the lookout for in your OKR program?

> *We are what we repeatedly do. Excellence, then, is not an act, but a habit.*

 Aristotle

As mentioned in the previous chapter, the PEEL Cycle is the best way to implement, manage, and reset OKRs. PEEL stands for **Plan, Execute, Engage, and Learn**.

This cycle addresses all of the key components and needs of a healthy OKR program. Across the board, experts and consultants can agree that the process of *planning, executing, engaging,* and *learning* addresses the demands of the OKR framework.

It is imperative to realize that OKR is not a single activity but an activity system. The best way to think of your OKR journey is to imagine riding a vehicle that runs on four wheels. All these four wheels must be operating in a coordinated manner to ensure you get to your destination. Similarly, each stage of the PEEL Cycle must be addressed in order to get the best results from your OKR program.

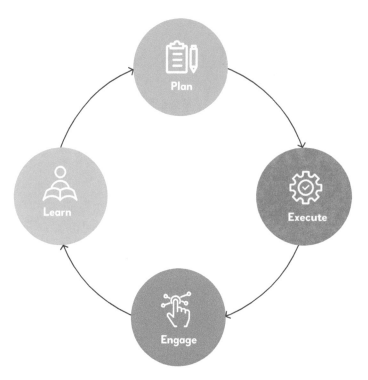

Figure 9.1: The four stages of the PEEL Cycle, which address all the components of a healthy OKR program: Planning, Executing, Engaging, and Learning.

To stick with the analogy of a vehicle, think back to when you first started driving. Everything in the car probably felt unfamiliar, and you had to focus all your energy on making sure the car was in the right gear, you turned on your blinker when you needed to, and you were obeying all traffic laws. Over time, though, these things became second nature. You were eventually able to listen to music or podcasts while you drove, and chat with your passengers with ease— all while driving safely and accurately to your destination.

Similarly, when you first start with OKRs, it might take a lot of concentration and effort to ensure that you are hitting all of the requirements for success— like planning weekly or biweekly meetings, completing check-ins, reviewing PPP reports, and resetting OKRs. However, over time, this will feel like a natural part of your daily life at work.

That is not to say that nothing will go wrong; even well-developed OKR programs can face a number of issues.

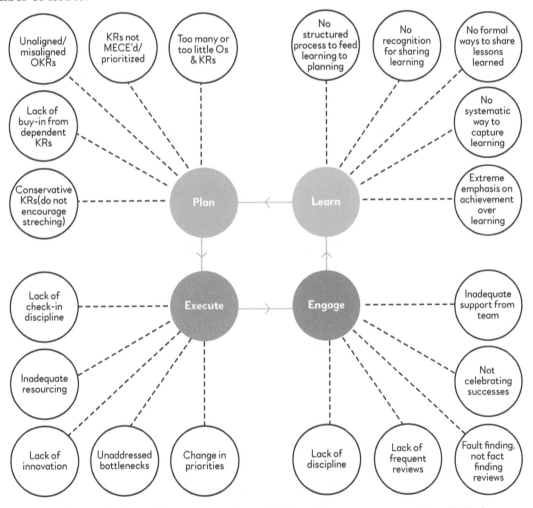

Figure 9.2: *The red flags you must be on the lookout for at every stage of the PEEL Cycle that could derail your OKR program.*

When it comes to the problems you face during your OKR journey, it's best not to think of them as issues that could cause failure. Instead, these are called red flags that you can look out for as warning signs that something is amiss and not operating at its fullest potential. If you don't address these red flags appropriately, they could lead to bigger problems— including getting discouraged with OKRs, and giving up the framework altogether.

Some of these red flags may seem generic and not specific to OKRs. However, they do have an OKR angle in most cases. In other cases where there is no direct connection to OKRs, it is essential to know that OKRs will not solve that problem. As discussed earlier, OKRs are a way of doing business, and the framework will not magically turn your business into an industry-leading company.

Let's take a look at the red flags at each stage of the PEEL Cycle. These four areas are strategically ordered by the perceived level of importance in most OKR programs. Most companies pay more attention to planning, slightly less attention to execution, and even less to engagement and learning. But in reality, all of these stages are equal. They all must be given the same level of attention and emphasis to make your OKR program successful.

Figure 9.3: *The four stages of the PEEL cycle repeat every quarter, with each learning step leading into the next quarter's planning step.*

Planning Red Flags

Planning is the first step in OKRs. A trip without a plan is a trip to nowhere. Many OKR practitioners and softwares emphasize planning over other functions. We have seen many businesses equate OKR planning to OKR practice, which is not true. They tend to put a ton of focus on planning and then believe that they are practicing OKRs.

While many may think that planning is their strong suit in their OKR implementations, these are red flags that you should be aware of to ensure that you successfully navigate this stage of the OKR cycle and avoid planning pitfalls.

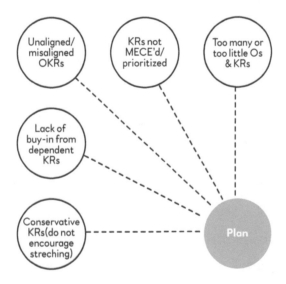

Too Many or Too Few Os and KRs

Ideally, you should have 3 to 5 Objectives with 3 to 5 Key Results for each Objective at each level or sector of the company. So, company-level OKRs should not exceed 5, and the number of OKRs for each department or team should also not exceed 5.

In one version of this red flag, you may have too few objectives and an insufficient amount of key results per objective. In another version, you may have too many objectives and too many key results per objective.

Both of these scenarios violate the focus principle of OKRs. If you have too many OKRs, you tend to have a diluted focus. And because of that, you will not have time to achieve everything that matters.

Having too few objectives might not be a focus problem, but it is more of a commitment problem, which can result in a lack of focus.

KR is Not MECE'd or Prioritized

While key results may be progressing on your tracking sheet or software, you may notice that the objective is not actually being achieved in your organization. The root of this issue is that your key results are not comprehensive or prioritized.

When trying to create key results, companies usually come up with a list that is not prioritized and often not even complete. If you have defined three to five key results that don't aptly fulfill the demands of the objective, your progress will be hollow.

Follow the MECE principle: key results should be mutually exclusive and collectively exhaustive. So, the key results you define for your objective must not overlap with one another, and they must collectively achieve the objective without leaving out any important factors that could affect the objective.

Without following these key result rules, you might complete your key results, but your objective itself will not be achieved.

Unaligned or Misaligned OKRs

Alignment is one of the core principles of the OKR methodology. Many users remember to prioritize this as they set corporate, department, team, and individual-level OKRs. Despite an emphasis on alignment, you might have a handful of OKRs that are not aligned with others above or below their level. A few unaligned OKRs is not necessarily a red flag. However, having a majority of unaligned OKRs, or all unaligned OKRs, presents an issue. This means that your organization's teams are not working together towards common goals, but instead they are operating in silos. While individual sectors of the business might achieve their OKRs, the overarching company goals will go unfulfilled, or only partially fulfilled.

Meanwhile, misaligned OKRs signal chaos and confusion. It should be clear why one OKR is aligning with another. Alignment for the sake of checking a box has the potential to upend your OKR program with miscalculated progress and a lack of clarity. If OKRs are completely unrelated, that should be an indicator that you need to set different OKRs that address the priorities of the company and departments more directly.

Lack of Buy-in from Dependent Key Results

Different business functions in a company depend on each other to accomplish the objectives of the company. When your organization is bigger and more spread out, dependencies are more pronounced, and the need to adequately negotiate, clarify, and agree on commitments increases.

Dependencies signal that in order to achieve your OKRs, you will need somebody else to keep their end of the bargain. In order to be successful, you need to have adequate conversations with them beforehand and ensure that the dependencies are clearly understood. There should be a mutual commitment to completing OKRs on schedule so that you can both accomplish your goals.

A common misunderstanding many users have in the early days of their OKR implementation is that once you set your Os and KRs, you are automatically assured of the other departments' commitments. There are simply no such guarantees, and if you do not have buy-in or commitment from other key stakeholders, the success of your OKR is at risk. Once you achieve commitments from departments or teams that you depend on, you need to regularly track those OKRs to ensure that you are aware of their progress and challenges.

Conservative Key Results

Success with OKRs is not just about the number of Objectives and Key Results you set, but also the nature of your Objectives and Key Results and the target you are trying to achieve.

For example, if you had 40 million new users last year, you should set an ambitious goal for this year– such as 90 million new users. This aims to more than double your success from last year. If you set a conservative target, like 60 million users, that isn't necessarily pushing your team to its limits, especially if 40 million users is the norm.

As a business leader, you must come up with ways to prevent these conservative key results. Attainable, safe key results are a clear violation of one of the OKR framework's important principles, which is to set stretch goals that push your team further than they think is possible.

The best way to overcome this problem is to stay aggressive, but be realistic. There should be a logic behind the "achievability" of the numbers. It cannot be just based on blind hope. We recommend following the SMART principle of goal setting, which requires goals to be **S**pecific, **M**easureable, **A**chievable, **R**ealistic, and **T**ime-bound.

Execution Red Flags

Now, let's take a look at the five red flags you need to watch out for while in the Execute stage of the PEEL Cycle.

Lack of Check-in Discipline

A lack of check-in discipline might seem trivial, but this is the number one problem reported by many OKR champions. Companies and teams must take check-ins seriously in order for OKRs to succeed. They have to check-in on time, as well as provide appropriate supporting information as to:

- What was achieved?

- What was not achieved?

- What did they learn over that period?

So, it is not just about reporting a number. It is about checking in with adequate supporting information. This information is what enables managers to help individuals with any roadblocks they are facing, and keeps the entire company informed about the progress of OKRs.

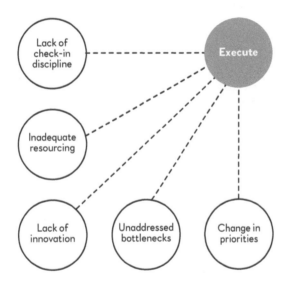

Check-ins have to become habitual. An organization should be committed to making this a habit. Software reminders can certainly help get check-ins done on time, but the importance of these check-ins must be reinforced by the culture of the company.

If your team does not make quality check-ins on time, OKRs will not be accurate reflections of organizational progress, and they will become essentially useless. Your OKR program won't take off if you have tracking problems like this.

Inadequate Resourcing

Resourcing, in this context, refers to all kinds of resources— not just people. Every type of resource must be understood and analyzed. If you have an infinite amount of every resource you need, you probably do not need OKRs. But infinite resources simply is not a reality for organizations.

Understanding what resources you have at your disposal, what goals you need to achieve, and how your resources can be used to help achieve them is a very important part of successfully executing your OKRs.

There will always be resource constraints, but it's up to you to find a way to apply the resources you do have in the most effective way possible.

As an organization, you must put your money where your mouth is. You cannot set a target to get 90 million users in a year, but not back that goal up with the investments needed to achieve it— investments such as the appropriate tools, access to technology, and sufficient manpower. If a key result is under-resourced, it's a red flag and indicator that you will not be able to achieve it.

Lack of Innovation

Lack of innovation could be thought of as a unique type of "resource" problem, but in this context, we should consider the rigid processes teams might have in place that drive innovation out of their company.

A lack of innovation can be a cultural problem, a people problem, or a process problem. But the bottom line is that if you do not have innovative thinking, you have a severe problem.

Good OKRs will automatically push people to be more innovative. However, if your people are not prepared, you will end up with a team that simply says: "OKRs didn't work out".

You will not have a tracking problem, but you will end up with check-ins that are stuck in the same place. Your stretch goals will consistently fail. It is normal not to hit all your stretch goals, but if you do not reach any of them, or even get close, you should take a look at the way your company's culture may restrict innovation. Do your teams have sharing sessions? Is there an opportunity for employees to offer new ideas? Do managers tend to micromanage employees? If your innovation issue isn't solved, it can cause problems for your entire OKR program.

Unaddressed Bottlenecks

Bottlenecks exist in business processes. Unaddressed bottlenecks are a huge process issue. Your people get going, but they are blocked by a bunch of roadblocks or bottlenecks which they cannot address by themselves. They need help from management or other departments to get moving again, significantly hampering execution.

An important role that management needs to play in the OKR world is to get the field ready for the players. When you push your employees to "stretch," you need to have the same commitment to ensuring you do not leave your people hanging when it comes to offering support and solving problems.

Bottlenecks will impact outcomes, and if you do not help your team address the issue they're facing alone, you run the risk of stalled OKRs and a stagnant OKR program.

Change in Priorities

Change is the only constant in this world. So, changing priorities in your OKR program isn't unexpected, and it's also not necessarily a problem by itself. However, not recognizing that priorities have changed and failing to adjust your OKRs and alignments to address these new priorities will quickly derail your OKR program.

For example, you might have an OKR that you have been working towards. Then, one month into the quarter, your focus shifts to an urgent and critical project that you must spend the rest of the quarter working on. In this situation, you would ideally create new OKRs to reflect that change in priority, then push the current ones that you are working on into the backlog to revisit when you have the bandwidth.

If you see a shift in priorities during the quarter, you shouldn't resist it. Instead, adjust your OKRs to support these new priorities and make sure that this new goal is tracked correctly. Many times, people adjust their priorities but fail to adjust their OKRs as well. This can lead to the conclusion that the OKR program is not working. Changing priorities should be understood and communicated throughout the entire organization so that the company does not fall out of alignment.

If you do not account for changing priorities, your tracking will go haywire, and your team will be busy doing the things that they were told were their priorities, but will not actually be addressing the company's true priorities.

Engagement Red Flags

Now, let's look at the red flags you need to catch during the third stage of the PEEL Cycle, Engage.

Lack of Discipline

If you ask an expert what the number one problem with traditional goal-setting processes is, nine out of ten times they will say that you just forgot about the exercise after setting the goals.

If you want a successful OKR program, that is one mistake you absolutely cannot make. Setting OKRs and then deciding to do whatever you want is like setting a goal to lose 20 pounds, and then not following the diet and exercise routine necessary to succeed.

If you go through a rigorous process of setting your OKRs and then ignore them for the rest

of the quarter or year, you are better off without OKRs. Your team could be facing commitment issues or communication issues that you can work through, but if there is a lack of discipline when it comes to OKRs, you have something to worry about.

If you have a solid tracking process and system in place, this problem will surface early and can be corrected.

Lack of Frequent Reviews

As you may have started to realize, these red flags are interrelated, as you usually see in activity systems. If you conduct frequent reviews of your OKRs (at least weekly), many of the other red flags will vanish, or at least greatly diminish.

On the other hand, if you do not conduct reviews periodically, many other problems will be amplified.

If you have a managerial process where you review OKR progress regularly, say weekly, and encourage your next levels to do the same, your OKR program will soar. The business results you see will motivate you to make OKRs habitual.

Many times, teams use spreadsheets or KPI dashboards to review their key numbers. It makes sense; the most important information, all in one place. If you incorporate OKRs into your review process, you can stay up to date on all OKR progress updates and catch any issues before they derail your OKR program.

Fault-Finding, not Fact-Finding Reviews

We talked about frequent reviews that focus primarily on the quantitative side of your review process. Now let's look at the qualitative aspect of reviews.

There are many ways to conduct reviews. From an OKR standpoint, you are encouraged to stretch. But if you make the review process too much about problems and finger-pointing, it will dampen the mood and encourage a sandbagging culture, where your team sets easy targets, and no substantial progress is achieved.

The reviews should focus on identifying and removing bottlenecks, dependencies, and other constraints to plow through and move forward. Identify resource shortages and either recognize or help solve the deficit. Focus efforts on finding information that can help improve OKR progress and achievement, rather than finding out who dropped the ball.

Short reviews focused on solving problems is the best way to make your OKR program successful.

The tone of your review can easily make people recoil and go into the sandbagging mode. Maintain a positive, encouraging tone.

Not Celebrating Successes

As a leader or manager, you must strive to create a positive culture. When you hold performance reviews, it can be nerve-wracking for employees and cause a lot of negativity and stress in your company.

So how do you create a positive culture? One of the easiest ways to do this is to start celebrating small successes.

One solution is starting off the week by congratulating the team on the progress they made in the last week, or taking a few minutes at the beginning of an existing meeting to recognize employees who have made great contributions to the team. This celebration can be a big confidence booster for those who are achieving their Key Results.

When you acknowledge an individual's effort, it motivates everyone and reinforces the fact that results get attention.

Inadequate Support from the Team

In order for OKRs to be successful, managers and key result owners must be attentive to their priorities. Additionally, other team members should be ready to support the key result owners, and are a vital part of OKR success.

You must find a way to ensure that the supporting team understands their role, even if they are not directly responsible for a key result. Teams must be ready to perform that role in order to deliver expected outcomes and help achieve OKRs. Without this understanding and commitment from the team, your OKR program could be derailed.

Learning Red Flags

The last stage of the PEEL cycle is learning. Learning is an area that is not emphasized in a lot of OKR implementations. Because of this, there are a number of potential problems that can pop up during this stage. Most companies using OKRs simply look at their OKR progress and call it a day, plunging into the next quarter without considering what could be improved. Let's take a look at the red flags in this stage of the PEEL cycle to help avoid a failed OKR program.

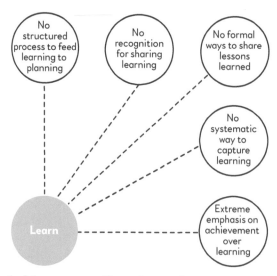

Extreme Emphasis on Achievement Over Learning

With this red flag, we are not saying that you should not focus on achievement. Achievement is significant. But if you focus on performance and completely ignore learning, you may have a problem.

Let us say you set out to go from the value "X" to "Y" of a KPI. But, at the end of the quarter, you are still stuck at "X". You have not moved the needle at all, or have made very little progress. Throughout the quarter, you tried dozens of different approaches to try to move your target, but none worked.

Instead of simply rolling over the OKR to the next quarter and blindly trying again, or even moving this key result to the backlog, you must find a way to record what did not work. That way, when others try to move the target next quarter, or you revisit the key result in the future, no one has to repeat the tactics that did not work. Even though you didn't make forward progress, you learned crucial information that your organization can benefit from.

Seeing results is great! But if you fail to achieve the results you aimed for, you should aim to understand why. This goes for your entire team. As long as you are sure that there was a sincere effort and attempt to make progress, it will be immensely beneficial to document employee learnings to set the company up for future success.

No Systematic Way to Capture Learnings

As part of your key results progress log, you should be able to document your learning. If you do not have a systematic way to capture the lessons you've learned from your OKR progress, how is your team supposed to grow?

A learning log or system is a crucial part of a successful OKR program. If you have a centralized learning log that is accessible to everyone, you will be able to promote a culture of learning, which is key to your OKR program's success. Without a learning log of some kind, there's a good chance that your OKR program will not develop and mature how you want it to, effectively stunting your success.

No Formal Way to Share Lessons Learned

Assuming you have a learning log, you should have a way to share your learnings formally. As a company, you should prioritize learning opportunities and make a point to share experiences that help one another grow.

You must promote knowledge-sharing sessions or brown bag sessions as appropriate to share success, failures, and learnings from the failure. It is challenging to create a "safe to fail" culture. Holding meetings for the express purpose of sharing lessons learned will help establish that culture.

No Recognition for Sharing Learning

Like celebrating successes, you should celebrate learning. If you do not recognize the effort behind documenting and sharing knowledge, your employees will not be motivated to document and share it in the first place. You must make it easy to share learning, especially when it comes to employee failures or roadblocks.

Establish a process to promote learning and sharing, and make a point to appreciate and recognize individual employees that share their knowledge. It takes a lot of courage for employees to admit that they failed, but this is ultimately how the team can help one another grow. You should aim to make people feel as comfortable as possible. The organization should create a culture that not only accepts failure, but recognizes and appreciates employees who share their learnings.

Obviously, you cannot build a company with failures. But when employees do fail, you must make a point to maximize the learning opportunities that come along with it. That way, next time your employees approach a certain problem or aim for a goal, they have the knowledge to help boost their chances of success.

No Structured Process to Feed Learning to Planning

Ideally, you will want your organization to:

- Tolerate faults and errors

- Recover quickly from failure

- Avoid repeating the same mistake twice

How do you ensure all this? The solution is to use a structured process that helps your team transition from the learning stage of the PEEL cycle to the planning stage. Whatever your team has learned in one quarter must be reviewed and taken into account when planning for the next quarter. The Reflect & Reset process makes learning a necessary step when setting your OKRs. Learnings can be through weekly reviews, brown bag sessions, audits conducted by consultants, or any other method that works for your company and provides a catalogue of learnings you can refer back to when it comes time to plan next quarter's OKRs.

Ensure that you allocate time and resources to institutionalize learning and channel that learning towards the next planning cycle.

Final Thoughts

As mentioned in the introduction, these red flags are just that— flags. They alert you that something may be amiss in your OKR program, and signal that it's time to evaluate your processes and make changes before your team gets derailed. Be vigilant about recognizing red flags when you see them, and make a point to resolve issues so that your team can remain focused on executing their OKRs. When you are proactive about resolving issues, you will have a more impactful and effective OKR program that keeps employees engaged, educated, and focused on what matters most for your company's success.

What red flags should you be on the lookout for in your OKR program?

10

What are the signs that your OKR program has matured and is running well?

There are always visible signs to tell if something is successful, or if it's headed in the opposite direction. This especially applies to the OKR framework. There are ways to tell when you and your team are doing something right. These signs are just as important to be aware of as red flags, because when you can identify the things you're doing well, you can replicate them and build a better understanding of the OKR framework in your company.

So, to help you identify the signals that things are going right in your team, let's take one last look at the PEEL Cycle and the hints that you might see in each stage that will let you know you're headed in the right direction.

P: Plan

The first step in the PEEL cycle is Plan.

It is important to know what you are doing correctly early in your OKR program because

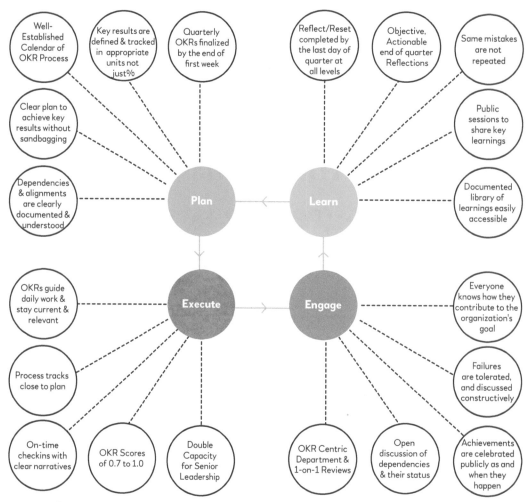

Figure 10.1: *An image of the PEEL Cycle and the signals you might see at each stage that help you realize what you're doing right.*

when you have a strong foundation, it is easier to bring that strength into your next steps. Planning is a process that happens each and every quarter, so cataloguing what's going right will help you build your expertise fast.

Your Quarterly OKRs are Finalized by the End of the First Week

When you are brand new to OKRs, finalizing your quarterly OKRs by the end of your first week can seem like a daunting task. You might not yet have a clear sense of what you would like to achieve for the entire quarter.

However, when you plan your OKRs in your second quarter, you have learned a little more. Then, in your third quarter, this process might go even more smoothly.

By your fourth quarter, you might have developed a rhythm or cadence with which you can plan clear OKRs at all levels— from company-wide to individual.

It is important to finalize your quarterly OKRs within the first week of your new quarter. If you are doing this with your OKR implementation, there doesn't have to be a lot of tension or discussion about your goals.

Everyone is on the same page, and there is probably very little internal friction or arguments for the lack of clarity or a loose understanding of dependencies and alignments.

If you have your OKRs defined by the end of the first quarter, this is one sign that your OKR program has matured and is running smoothly.

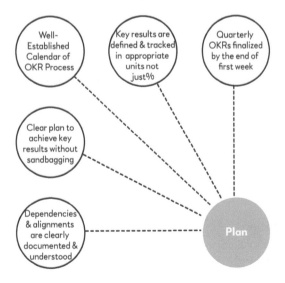

Key Results are Defined and Tracked in Appropriate Units- Not Just Percentages

The second sign of a successful program is that your key results are clearly defined and tracked using the appropriate units— not just measured in terms of the percentage completed.

Generally, when people first start out creating Key Results, they tend to use the percentage-tracked key result type because it doesn't require much forethought when it comes to tracking progress. Then, after some time, you gain the confidence and understanding to graduate to more concrete, tangible tracking units.

For example, instead of having a key result to "Improve customer satisfaction score by 40%," you would create a key result to "Increase customer satisfaction score from 80 to 95".

It is a more specific, useful way to define your key results, and indicates maturity in your understanding and creation of OKRs.

A Well-Established Calendar of your OKR Process

Having a well-established calendar indicating your OKR process is a great sign that you are doing something right. Having a clear idea of your quarter and visualizing how frequently you would like to hold specific meetings is incredibly essential to success with OKRs.

Here are some good indicators that you have a well-established calendar:

- Monday OKR status meetings

- Weekly progress plans

- Friday check-ins

- Frequent status updates

Some events and meetings might be held once a month or once a quarter. For example, you could designate every first or third Wednesday as a day for your team to celebrate goal-setting successes or do lunch-and-learn Q&A sessions.

Monthly meetings can and should be increasingly local, getting down to the department and team levels.

Once a quarter, you might have a company "town-hall" meeting in a larger setting. Here, you can talk about achievements, failures, lessons learned, and even awards or recognitions at the division or business unit levels.

Clear Plan to Achieve the Committed Key Results– Without Sandbagging

With OKRs, you should be encouraging yourself and others to stretch. Because some of the goals you are setting might be "stretch goals," you could fall into a pattern of dreaming big without actionable steps to achieve that dream.

To succeed, you need a plan– a business is not run solely on stretch goals.

You will want to have a precise achievement level understood before beginning and a clear plan for delivering at that level. However, it is better to strike a balance between achievable and aspirational to maintain clarity and possibility without promoting sandbagging.

Dependencies and Alignments are Clearly Documented and Understood

Dependencies and alignments are an essential part of your planning process because you need to understand how your highest corporate-level OKRs might flow down to the next level, your departments, and then to teams and individuals.

The connections need to be clearly understood by everyone involved. If this is happening, then it is an excellent sign that you're on track in your planning process.

It also includes dependencies between teams. If one team needs to deliver X, they need to recognize that they need other teams to provide Y and Z to fulfill their objective.

Documenting and understanding dependencies and alignments is the last sign that you are doing something right in your planning process.

E: Execute

When you have a steady foundation that has been built through the planning process, you are ready to continue to the next stage of the PEEL cycle: **executing your OKRs**.

Having a clear idea of what signs show that you are headed in the right direction can help you find success during this stage. What are the signs you are doing something right?

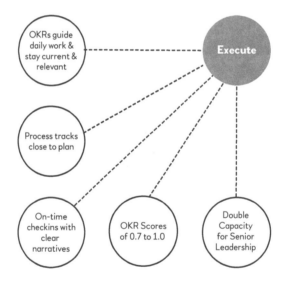

OKRs Guide Daily Work and Stay Current & Relevant

OKRs are not just crucial to the big picture; they should also guide everyday work. Suppose OKRs stay current and relevant to what is happening in your company's day-to-day operations. In that case, that is an excellent sign that your OKR program is mature and that your OKRs are being executed properly.

Sometimes, OKRs are formulated at the beginning of the quarter, but by week four or five, the key results must change, as they lose relevance and importance.

Sometimes, a company experiences a shift in priorities in the middle of a quarter – but when this happens, your work-tracking should reflect that. It should never be the case that work is irrelevant to the completion of your OKRs.

Progress Tracks Close to Plan

Another indicator of success in this stage of the OKR progress is how closely your progress is tracking to your original expectations. There are situations where a specific key result could get a stunted start– for example, no progress for the first six weeks.

You could reason that you might get to it later in the quarter– but this introduces an unnecessary sense of anxiety surrounding this goal.

It is better to see your KRs progressing on schedule, especially if this is not an individual KR, but rather a team or departmental KR, or a KR with dependencies.

On-Time Check-Ins with Clear Narratives

The next signal that the *"execution"* portion of your PEEL process is going well is that your check-ins are consistent, and they paint a very clear narrative. It is perhaps the most important signal that your OKRs can give. This is the element that lets you know what was completed, and what got left out.

It's the very baseline of your key result progress, asking the big question: "What did we get done?"

Once you see this, you can figure out if there are any gaps, determine a game plan for making up work, and get your team and your goal back on track.

OKR Scores of 0.7 to 1.0

OKR scoring at the end of the quarter will indicate how well you did with this aspect of the execution process.

At the end of the quarter, you should see an OKR score between 0.7 to 1.0. In some cases, you might dip below that. However, if you are seeing this score at the end of the quarter, it's a good sign that you are succeeding in this stage of the PEEL cycle.

Doubled Capacity for Senior Leadership

An interesting sign of success that you could see in this stage of the OKR process is the increase in capacity for Senior Management. This extra time and room in Senior Management's work lives would leave them room to focus on even more prominent, bolder ideas to implement within the company.

Now, this symptom is subtle – it is not a flashy, obvious sign that you will see all of the time. However, when it occurs, it is a great sign that you are doing something right with your OKR program. When Senior Management does not have to spend their time chasing down employees and following up with people to organize all the company's tasks, they have more time to focus on bigger-picture items.

When this happens, a weekly review is sufficient to cover a lot of ground and updates with the team. Getting to this point might take time and effort; however, it is an obvious sign that your OKR program is progressing successfully.

E: Engage

An essential element of the OKR process is **Engagement**. Not just with OKRs– even if everyone is doing their check-ins, there should be a broader, more unified engagement with OKRs through monthly meetings. When executed correctly, OKRs will seamlessly integrate into your day-to-day work life. Let's look at some signs that the PEEL cycle's **engagement stage** is going right.

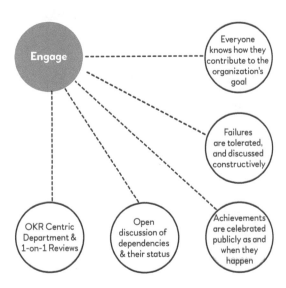

OKR-Centric Department and 1-on-1 Reviews

A standard pillar of Employee Engagement is reviews. These can be at varying points throughout the quarter. Some managers might want to have weekly, biweekly, or monthly meetings to get up to date and put everyone on the same page.

Additionally, having 1-on-1s with your direct employees is an essential element of engagement. OKRs should be a big part of your daily, weekly, and monthly reviews. If they are, this is a great way to tell that the engagement stage of the PEEL cycle is going well– and your OKR program is mature and healthy.

Open Discussion on Dependencies & their Statuses

From an engagement standpoint, open discussion about dependencies and their statuses should be a large part of daily or weekly conversations.

Chances are, your OKRs have both dependencies and alignments– both require communication. Assumptions can be dangerous and cause your team to get side-tracked. Everyone has to check-in with one another and stay updated.

Suppose everyone in your team participates in the check-in process and has open conversations– then the progress is clear to all. In that case, that is a great sign that your OKR program is running smoothly and efficiently.

Achievements are Publicly Celebrated as, and When, they Happen

While many of these indicators are necessary, this one in particular is very significant because employee recognition is a large part of employee engagement. Both successes and failures must be recognized.

You do not want low morale to negatively affect your environment. Celebrating achievements– small, large, noteworthy, or everyday– as they come is vitally important. Doing this in your OKR program can help you maintain a very positive and improvement-oriented culture.

Failures are Tolerated, and Discussed Constructively

Failure is a meaningful thing to discuss because this might not feel like a sign of success. How could failure be an indicator of doing something right?

It is not so much about the failure itself as it is about the reaction to failure. When people try something new, there is not always going to be leaps-and-bounds of progress.

However, learning is a part of the execution. The effort that goes into failure needs to be expended to come out better on the other side.

If you have a healthy culture that tolerates failure and finds solutions in a constructive, discussion-based manner, it is a sign that your OKR program is going well.

Everyone is Aware of their Contribution to the Organization's Goals

This sign of success is critical to know about because of what it indicates. Goals throughout a company are usually informed by the goals at a higher level in the hierarchy.

No matter how far down the chain of command they are, any team member or individual in the company should see how they are a significant, impactful contributor to the organization's OKRs. Alignments should be clearly linked to show who is contributing, and in what ways.

This connection to higher-level goals isn't always tangible. Instead, it's more of an understanding that team members have as they execute their goals. When they know how they fit into the hierarchy or make a meaningful impact on the overall Objective, it creates a sense of pride and belonging. It automatically boosts company-wide morale. If an employee can comprehend how their completion of task X fits into company goal Y, your OKR program runs smoothly and successfully.

L: Learning

Learning is a very valuable part of the PEEL cycle. Arguably, it is what makes this process worth it, because it enables you to learn lessons from the OKR cycle that you can use moving forward.

You Have an Easily-Accessible Library of Learnings

A documented library of all the lessons you have learned through the OKR process, as well as your end-of-quarter reflections, is a sign of success that you should be thrilled to see in your organization.

Not only is this useful for current employees, but it can act as an orientation booklet for new hires, who can now gain a clear understanding of their new role by looking at the OKR history. Instead of having to go through failures to learn lessons, employees can simply read through the documented lessons and benefit from the shared company knowledge. They can build on the company's prior knowledge so that they do not repeat the same mistakes.

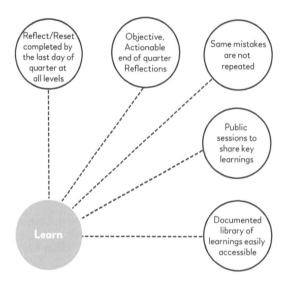

Regular, Public Sessions to Share Key Learnings

You should have meetings on a monthly basis where people can openly share the important things they learned and what mistakes they made during the OKR cycle.

By sharing mistakes and overcoming them, there can be a collective sense of understanding and learning. Others can use these suggestions and warnings to move forward in their own goals and make progress.

Same Mistakes are Not Repeated

How a person reacts to and tolerates failures says a lot about them. Being about to learn from those failures says even more.

Companies doing well with their OKR programs will not have many repeated failures amid their employees. If employees can share what goes wrong with one another and deal with that failure, then everyone will be better off.

A limited number of repeated mistakes indicates good communication within a company, and an open environment to talk and help. Keeping a catalog of lessons learned is a way that one employee can share with an entire company and help everyone understand and improve.

Objective, Actionable End-of-Quarter Reflections

When you begin a reflect-and-reset session, it should be a highly objective, action-oriented reflection on the quarter. You don't want to flood your reflection with subjective opinions or have discussions that don't substantially contribute to your evaluation of your quarter.

Make reflections clear. Discuss when you tried and failed, as well as when you were successful. Writing clear reflections can help future team members down the line to learn from your mistakes and build on your progress.

Reflect & Reset Complete by the Last Day of the quarter at All Levels

End-of-quarter objectives should be completed every quarter without fail. It is essential to take your time with these reflections. Do not be afraid to start them a week or ten days before the end of the quarter.

Starting early will give you ample time to thoughtfully comment on what you did right in the quarter and where you could have improved. Also, it helps you figure out if you are going to reset some of your Key Results or modify and continue them.

These signs of success are all indicators that you are working with a healthy and mature OKR program. Recognizing these characteristics in your program at each stage of the **PEEL cycle** indicates a reason to celebrate and keep moving forward with ambitious goals.

What are the signs that your OKR program has matured and is running well?

Conclusion

In this final installment of the OKR Program series, you learned how to schedule your quarter with OKRs, how to prioritize your goals, techniques to promote OKR best practices, and the signs you need to look out for to ensure that your program is on track. With this information and knowledge, combined with what you have learned in the first two installments of this series, you are now ready to embark on your OKR journey. Best of luck on your OKR implementation and beyond!

Remember:

- OKR is a goal management system used by teams to collaborate and achieve stretch goals through a framework that requires regular check-ins, feedback, continuous learning, collaboration and problem-solving.

- OKRs are simple yet powerful as they are useful for startups and large corporations to execute their strategy with focus and alignment.

- Objectives (the O in OKR) are qualitative, inspirational, time-bound goals to be executed by a team or an individual.

- Key Results (KR), on the other hand, quantify the OKR's objective and break it down to specific metrics that can be used to measure the achievement of the Objectives.

- While there are hundreds of management theories and frameworks– the power of OKRs comes from the widespread adoption and proven success stories across the globe. Objectives and key results help companies and teams to excel in execution.

- The critical elements of OKRs tie into each other. During the planning process, teams are forced to drop all but 3-5 Objectives. This helps teams stay focused.

- Similarly, as Corporate OKRs are cascaded to department and team levels, there is stronger alignment, and a sense of employee empowerment throughout the organization.

- Transparent scoreboards, regular reviews, and feedback cycles provide the framework the necessary support and rigor to excel in achieving stretch goals.

No wonder OKRs have been an incredible tool powering some of the most innovative companies of this century.